Can War be Eliminated?

Christopher Coker

CAN WAR BE ELIMINATED?

polity

First published in 2014 by Polity Press

Polity Press
65 Bridge Street
Cambridge CB2 1UR, UK

Polity Press
350 Main Street
Malden, MA 02148, USA

ISBN-13: 978-0-7456-7922-8
ISBN-13: 978-0-7456-7923-5 (pb)

A catalogue record for this book is available from the British Library.

Typeset in 11 on 15 pt Sabon by
Servis Filmsetting Ltd, Stockport, Cheshire
Printed and bound in Great Britain by Clays Ltd, St Ives

The publisher has used its best endeavours to ensure that the URLs for external websites referred to in this book are correct and active at the time of going to press. However, the publisher has no responsibility for the websites and can make no guarantee that a site will remain live or that the content is or will remain appropriate.

Every effort has been made to trace all copyright holders, but if any have been inadvertently overlooked the publisher will be pleased to include any necessary credits in any subsequent reprint or edition.

For further information on Polity, visit our website:
www.politybooks.com

War: thunder against it.
    Flaubert, *The Dictionary of Received Ideas*

Contents

Prologue

It is the summer of 1983 and Major-General Albert Stubblebine III, the US Army's recently appointed Chief of Intelligence, with no fewer than 16,000 soldiers under his direct command, finds himself confounded by his failure to walk through the wall of his office. One day, the ability to pass through office walls will be a common tool in intelligence gathering, he surmises, and when that day dawns it will surely herald a world without war.[1]

The story appears in *The Men Who Stare at Goats*, a book by Jon Ronson, which was later turned into a popular movie with George Clooney in the starring role. But the soldiers trained on the US Army's Parapsychology Program did not think they were precursors of peace. Large amounts of money were spent on parapsychology, both by the Soviet Union and by the United States, in the latter half of the Cold War in the vain attempt to reboot war for a new age. This is the dynamic of war: every time you think you have invented a technology that cannot be used, soon enough you find it can.

Parapsychological warfare may stretch the limits of the imagination, but does it necessarily stretch the limits of our understanding of war? The short answer is no. In truth the research was a sideshow of the Cold War – the Americans pushed on largely because the Russians took it seriously, and what an enemy takes seriously, you must too. As for the future, one psychic spy believes that the Chinese government is currently investing in parapsychological warfare in preparation for a future war against the United States.[2]

The programme aptly captures what Barbara Ehrenreich describes as war's iron grip on culture. She considers war to be a 'self-replicating pattern of behaviour'.[3] When considered as a 'self-programming cultural activity', it would appear to be one of the most robust social activities of all. Take the Serbian criminal groups who at the height of the conflict in the Balkans ran a profitable side-line in military tourism. For a fee, wealthy tourists could spend an afternoon sniping at the citizens of Sarajevo, lobbing mortar bombs into the marketplace of Mostar or firing artillery into a medium-sized city. The Russian avant-garde writer Edouard Limonov was actually captured on video enjoying this ultimate human safari. And then there were the American volunteers who joined paramilitary groups, claiming to be professional mercenaries, or ex-US Rangers, or even Green Berets. Many, in fact, only knew of war from what they had watched on TV. In other words, some people were prepared to go to great lengths, at some risk to themselves, to experience war. In this particular case, to invoke Clausewitz, we could say that war had become 'the continuation of tourism by other means'.

Even in cyberspace war is continuing to evolve in new and unexpected ways. Take Second Life, an on-line virtual world which was designed to help architects and digital designers to build virtual properties and which now offers an alternative life for those who have yet to get one. It mimics everything in the real world; it has its own economy and currency. A few years ago Nissan allowed its users to virtually test drive one of its new models on Second Life before it became available in the real world. But these kinds of developments have also generated a self-organized Second Life Liberation Army which has staged virtual world terrorist attacks against Nissan and other popular brand names. The point about virtual worlds is that they allow players to escape the bleakness and pointlessness of their own lives; players can play many roles, and even play at war, even though the designers never intended it to be part of the program.

In a word, war is remarkably resilient. It has always changed colour in the available light. War, wrote one of our most distinguished military historians, 'is a protean activity ... like disease, it exhibits the capacity to mutate, and it mutates fastest in the face of efforts to control or eliminate it'.[4] Most recently it has even regained a new lease of life in fresh dimensions, including cyberspace, while robotics promises to reduce its 'human space' still further. Defining resilience, maintain Andrew Zolli and Anne-Marie Healy, is complicated by the fact that the term means different things in different fields. In engineering it generally refers to the degree in which a structure can return to a baseline state after being disturbed. In psychology it signifies the capacity of an individual to deal effectively with trauma. In business it is often used to mean putting in place back-ups (of data and resources) to ensure continuous operation in the face of natural or man-made disasters. But Zolli and Healy's preferred definition is worth taking to heart: 'the capacity of a system, enterprise, or a person, to maintain its core purpose and integrity in the face of dramatically changed circumstances'.[5] Such has been the history of war since we emerged from the hunter-gatherer stage of our development, and there is no reason to doubt that war will prove any less resilient in the future. In this brief essay I will argue that, contrary to what many would argue, war is not pathological, any more than it is socially dysfunctional, and it most certainly is not just a bad idea that we can cash in for a better one, peace. It has played such a central role in the human story because it is embedded in our cultural evolution and, unfortunately, this is likely to remain the case for some time yet.

1

Evolution

About 100,000 years ago human beings began to evolve in a way that was not true of any other species – our social practices began to replicate, mutate and accumulate just as genes had been doing for billions of years. The key was our own exceptional neural plasticity, which significantly increases our adaptability. It is the foundation for the skills which are unique to us such as language, self-awareness and self-control. The term we use for the ability to pass on social skills such as collaborating and communicating via speech or Facebook is a very simple one: culture.

In *Darwin's Cathedral*, David Sloan-Wilson offers a very persuasive example of cultural evolution with respect to religion, one of the most important cultural phenomena of all. He describes it as an adaptive product whose function is to facilitate co-operation in larger units. Religion, Wilson insists, appears to be 'designed' to minimize internal competition within groups and maximize the competitive advantage of a particular group.[1] It establishes social norms as well as penalties against those who break them; it also promotes group selflessness – in binding people together it makes them put the group's interests ahead of their own.

The same dynamic would appear to be also operative in the case of war. Like religion it had adaptive value – it protected us against the murderous in-fighting of tribal groups and it helped us to avoid characterizing out-groups as non-human, in contrast to the characterization of other tribes. The names that hunter-gatherer tribes call themselves tell their own story – 'the People', 'the Good Ones' or 'the Fully Complete Ones'. Primitive warfare is particularly murderous, for that reason, and mortality rates are astonishingly high. Some of the battles in hunter-gatherer societies have a death rate of 0.5% of the population per year. If that had been true of industrialized warfare in the twentieth century 2 billion people would have died instead of the 100 million who actually did.[2] Had that dynamic been maintained over the centuries you probably wouldn't be reading this book.

Generally speaking, the more co-operative a species is within the group, the more hostility there is between groups. When there is a very variegated society, such as in New Guinea, which has more than 800 languages, out-group enmity can be fierce. That is why Robert Wright believes that religion was essential for early states to keep war within bounds. The relationship between the two is a dialectical one. The gods (in his felicitous words) were 'geopolitical lubricants' who made possible rudimentary international law; divine authority policed treaties between tribes and later hereditary chiefdoms. The problem, of course, was that the gods also sanctioned war, and still do.[3] Think of the suicide bomber in today's Middle East. The point is that religion is still deeply entrenched in human life. Schopenhauer thought we would outgrow it as we do our childhood clothes, but the failure of the 'new atheism' to make much of an impact suggests that we need to go back to humanity's childhood to see why it still has 'an iron grip' on us all; and if that is true of religion, it is surely also true of war.

Now, of course, this is an unashamedly group selection thesis and it assumes that warfare is the natural state of human existence. Fortunately, however, group selection is now coming back into fashion after being challenged in the 1960s. The neo-Darwinian evolutionists who still reject it, claims Mary Midgley, have simply misread Darwin.[4] And although there are many anthropologists who still question whether aggression has always been rewarded and can often be inherited, here too the tide is turning (Jared Diamond's *The World until Yesterday* [2012] makes short work of the traditional idea that primitive societies are innately peaceful).

What is important about evolution is that it is an active agent in increasing the options, choices and possibilities of the different species, organisms or societies in which it is the life principle. It promotes among other things ubiquity, diversity and complexity. The fact that all three show continued development would suggest that war is continuing to evolve, and that it is unlikely to be eliminated until such time as its evolutionary possibilities have finally been exhausted.

Ubiquity

The evolution of war, writes Edward O. Wilson, was an auto-catalytic reaction that could not be halted by any people, because to attempt to reverse the process unilaterally would have been fatal.[5] 'War is not the best way of settling differences, but it is the only way of preventing them being settled for you' (G.K. Chesterton). Chesterton's words are well taken. An auto-catalytic reaction is something that gathers pace by feeding upon itself. It breeds, explodes and grows and it is facilitated by other attributes that are unique to humans – language, for one. Not one major power, empire or culture decided not to go into the war business, and not one so far has gone out of it. To have rejected war would have been as fatal as rejecting agriculture; the Mesolithic communities of Central Asia who did the latter were quickly side-lined by history. This may appear counter-intuitive but it is not. As Edward Luttwak puts it: 'The paradoxical language of strategy contradicts the logic of everyday life. It goes against all normal definitions of intelligence we have. It only makes sense if you understand the dialectic. If you want peace, prepare for war; if you actively want war, disarm yourself and then you'll get it.'[6]

Devoid of anti-social instincts we probably might have led a peaceful life, but that is not how we are designed biologically. Hobbes was quite right to tell us that war is central to the human condition and that its causes – competitiveness, diffidence (fear) and glory (honour) – are what make us human. We are instinctively territorial creatures whether we are laying claim to land, marking out a person as property, or, as in the last century, defining the limits of someone else's thoughts. The propensity to excel makes us sociable as well as competitive; it also makes us fearful of others who are competing against us. Finally, honour is programmed into us to amplify emotions such as pride, anger and love of kith and kin. We are prone to retaliate against those who would dishonour us. Honour is a social bond and winning it back a social obligation, and it is just as important today as it was in our prehistoric past (the only difference is that we have translated it into a new currency: credibility). War remains ubiquitous because we are still in thrall to our inherited biology, and from the first day that our ancestors threw a stone in anger, tools and then technology have enabled us to compete more successfully.

Paleoanthropologists tell us that our 'accelerated evolution' is techno-organic in nature; we developed so that we could use technology, and it is just so happens that technology has been determining our history as never before. At least 76 countries, for example, are developing some form of drone technology (and other non-state actors will follow the lead set by Hamas and Hizballah). It is not a very promising prospect given that even the United States is finding it difficult to adapt its traditional codes of warfare to the practice of war by remote control. Drones are evolving faster than our ability to understand how, legally and ethically, to employ them. Like Darwin's finches, they are evolving furiously to fill more and more operational niches, and creating new ones as they go.

Even nuclear weapons, the signature weapon of the twentieth century, may be coming back into fashion. In the 1960s 31 countries had nuclear weapons programmes; 22 chose to abandon them. But nuclear proliferation is back on the agenda. The principal lesson of the First Gulf War (1991) was that any country that does not wish to be attacked by the US should develop nuclear weapons. And there is now a global trade in nuclear material for states or non-state actors who wish to do precisely that. All of which merely confirms what we have always known: it is impossible to restrict technologies to 'the haves'. What Marvin Minsky calls the 'have-laters' are merely waiting in the wings.[7]

Diversity

Human cultural traditions which are ubiquitous promote different ways of performing the same task. Imagine war without cultural diversity. Max

Brooks gives us a vivid example of one in his best-selling book *World War Z* (2011). The novel is constructed around a series of interviews with those who survived the Great Zombie War. So, what were the problems, an American general is asked, in dealing with zombies? World War Z was a total war, but not one with which human beings were familiar. No society is ever 100% committed to fight. There are always the old and the young, the pacifists and the Fifth Columnists, and the conscientious objectors and the fellow travellers. Not so, of course, in the case of zombies, who gave 100% commitment. All societies also have their limits; few will risk total destruction. Zombies, unfortunately, had no limits of endurance. They didn't surrender, or negotiate, or give up the fight because of low morale.

So how did humanity eventually prevail? Only by re-thinking the rules of war and putting themselves back in touch with styles of war which had long gone out of fashion. The Europeans retreated to their old fortifications, fortresses and castles, as centres of resistance (zombies cannot climb walls). The American military had to learn new skills, or, rather, older ones long since abandoned. It had to re-introduce the classic eighteenth-century firing line, with one line active in front, and the other in reserve behind. And it was able to combine this with modern technology, using downlinks from satellites and recon drones to monitor zombie groups as they swarmed. Fortunately, for the rest of us, the zombies never had a chance.[8]

Brooks' book contains enough wisdom to have persuaded the Commandant of the US Naval War College to invite its author to speak to the senior officers about the Global War on Terror. But my reason for citing it is to point out that zombies are all alike. Like us they have needs and appetites; unlike us they don't have desires. They don't have culture, and that makes all the difference. War varies across cultures, as language does. Language evolved just once but languages have been evolving all the time since then. War evolved just once, as well, but ways of warfare show amazing diversity. As the linguist Noam Chomsky showed, all human languages share some basic structural similarities – a universal grammar. So does war; its different registers – total and limited, regular and irregular – have continued to unfold historically.

And there is another evolutionary dynamic at work. When the cultural environment changes, writes Daniel Dennett, a cultural born habit can evaporate overnight, powering a potent feedback cycle that speeds up evolution.[9] A vivid example is the Plains Indians in the nineteenth century, who were willing to purchase guns but only in defence of an already endangered form of life, not to survive the challenge by adapting their traditions. Mark Pagel calls it 'shape-shifting' via social learning. There is no shape-shifting in nature. The practices and behaviour of chimpanzees (even when they go on raids) have remained the same for 300,000 years. We began adapting because we had to – when we moved out of the African savannah. Social learning allowed us to build complex societies as we selected the best from a range of options.[10] It is a particularly good example, writes Matt Ridley in his book *The Rational Optimist* (2011), of 'ideas having sex'. What is remarkable is that this asymmetry is as entrenched in war today as it was 150 years ago when the Plains Indians last rode into battle.

In tracking the cultural diversity of war in the last 200 years military experts have identified different 'generations'. In the most recent of these, Fourth Generation Warfare (4GW), high-tech powers face elusive and technologically inferior opponents who are both innovative and inventive, nevertheless, at using all available networks, political, economic, social and military, to achieve their own ambitions. (Those ambitions, in turn, may not be primarily political; the actors may be agents of a market of violence seeking to maximize financial profit by leveraging technology). Fifth Generation Warfare (5GW), meanwhile, is about to come on stream:

> If traditional war centred on an enemy's physical strength and 4GW on his moral strength, the Fifth Generation of war would focus on his intellectual strength. The Fifth Generation War might be fought with one side not knowing who it is fighting. Or even, a brilliantly executed 5GW might involve one side being completely ignorant that there ever was a war. It's like the old question, what was the perfect robbery: we'll never know, because in a perfect robbery the bank would not know that it was robbed.[11]

Given that on average it takes 300 days or more before a company knows its computers have been hacked, 5GW may already be here. The Chinese military has been hacking into the Pentagon's computers for some years now; the 'Cool War' it is called – one that is militarily more costly than the Cold War, but one which may never go 'hot'.

Even in technological backwaters like the Congo, where you might expect to find no innovations or new techniques, war is evolving there too. In February 2010 the UN approved the first Special Representative on sexual violence in conflict because of the way that for the first time in history rape is becoming a weapon, as well as a by-product of war. Rape in the East Congo today is now so extensive that it is defined by some experts as 'genocide by attrition'. Elsewhere in the world, jihadists and insurgents have also been remarkably innovative – their strength lies in their open-sourced structure that allows for decision-making cycles that are much shorter than those of state militaries. Culture, we can be sure, will continue to shape the development and diffusion of military knowledge, producing indigenous adaptations that are difficult to predict.

Historians used to think that in wiping out many different cultural ways of war in the course of the nineteenth century, including the Zulu and Native American, the West had forced the 'rest' to copy western techniques. But copying is not always emulation and much of the world that the West 'disarmed' a century or so ago is now 'rearming'. We should remember that the era of western military superiority only really dates from 1820, a period that coincided not only with the industrial revolution, but also with the decline of much of the non-western world. For most of human history western armies lagged far behind their Chinese (and even Indian) counterparts, and they may do so again in the future. If western economic dominance is on the wane, the same may be true of America's military dominance. In recent years, writes Andrew Bacevich, opponents of western military might have employed a panoply of techniques to undercut the apparent advantages of high-tech conventional forces. 'The sun has set on the age of unquestioned Western military dominance. ... Bluntly, the East has solved the riddle of the Western way of war.'[12]

Complexity

The world is full of complex structures that are the outcome of a small number of simple, symmetrical laws and that is possible because the outcomes of the laws of nature need not possess the symmetrical properties of the laws themselves. The laws can be the same everywhere; the outcomes need not be. At first glance, we might think war is not an especially complex activity. Wars resemble each other, writes Michael Howard, far more than they resemble any other human activity (i.e., they are fought in special elements of danger, fear and confusion). In all wars bodies of men try to impose their will on others by violence. And in all wars events occur which are inconceivable in any other field of experience.[13] Even so, the differences are also very great, and as a military historian Howard has spent much of his life charting them. They give war a different character every era, without challenging what Clausewitz called its true nature.

Indeed, war itself is a product of the social complexity of life. Take, for example, 'the human web', which has grown from the thin localized webs that characterized agricultural communities 12,000 years ago, through the denser, more interactive metropolitan web of the first civilizations, to the digitalized global web that today envelops the entire world. Hunter-gatherer societies were comparatively simple in structure. Farming villages were more complex. Early civilizations were more complex still because they encouraged specialization – the division of labour. Today's cosmopolitan web is only made possible by massive energy capture – the electricity that allows for the transmission and storage of vast streams of data.

But there is a price to pay for integration, which is where war comes into the picture. Complex societies do not just co-exist with simple ones. They tend to destroy and absorb the surviving elements. Complexity seems to have conferred a greater competitive advantage on some societies at the expense of others; those at the cutting edge tend to get a jump on others and appropriate their resources. Thus co-operation produces inequalities, and inequality would seem to be growing at a faster rate than ever.[14]

It is often argued, of course, that the 'in-group' is going global as various societies and peoples are drawn closer together in an intensified sense of shared experiences and common identities. But a more insidious dynamic is at work in the world at large. The 'information rich' are becoming separated from the 'information poor', two categories that have replaced the old 'haves' and 'have-nots' who were identified first, not by Marx, but by Aristotle. Today the 'low-techs' have been excluded from a labour market that is increasingly geared to the processing and consumption of information. And that could be dangerous because the only work many may be able to find may take the form of what economists call 'informal survivalism'. Simply to survive they may have to join criminal gangs, private armies, urban militias, warlords' retinues or terrorist groups. Most of them are to be found in the planet's 260,000 shanty towns, or densely packed slums (what Zygmunt Bauman, in *Wasted Lives* [2004], calls 'waste disposal units' for a vast, unemployed and unemployable mass of people: the cast-offs of late modernity, the 'collateral damage of globalization').

For the likely template of what is to come in the

future, think of the Mumbai bombings in 2008, when five two-man teams struck at the same time. In five separate attacks over two days the terrorists held a major world city hostage.[15.] The United States, meanwhile, has plans of its own. One day quite soon giant airships hovering overhead with up-to-date sensors will be able to engage in 'datamining' – the plan is eventually to 'digitalize' entire cities and so allow soldiers to see through walls (if not yet walk through them). Imagine, writes Peter Singer, the video game *Sin City* crossed with Google Earth.[16]

Metrowar – close combat in an urban landscape – is just over the horizon. If the evolutionary paradigm I have set out in this chapter is true, then we are surely forced to reach an inescapable conclusion. The twenty-first century may well not be as war-torn as the twentieth, but as long as war continues to evolve, its last chapter is not even close to being written.

2

Culture

We look to the future for a reason: to redirect our attention to the present. Future gazing 'is in effect a mirror process which only has one mirror: to improve our ability to change our so-called "future fitness"'.[1] War has done precisely that, I contend, which is why it is so resilient. But it is important to ask whether it is has lost – or is beginning to lose – its adaptive value. Perhaps, the only people it really benefits are its 'purveyors' – the warriors who derive their humanity from it, just as some would claim that the only 'good' that religion does is to institutions such as the priesthood. It is in the nature of war, Clausewitz suggested, to end up serving only itself, but a somewhat different understanding is that it can end up serving those who benefit from it the most. We could even conclude that just as people can be seen as DNA's way of producing other people and scholars can be seen as a library's way of creating new libraries, war is the way by which warriors reproduce themselves.

In some senses, writes Barbara Ehrenreich, war can be seen as a loose assemblage of algorithms or programs, in the computer sense of the term, for collective action. The idea that it is glorious to die for one's country, for example, was especially tenacious – and in some societies still is. In that respect, culture cannot always be counted upon to be on our side. It promotes some very bad ideas, as well as some very good ones. 'Insofar as it allows humans to escape the imperatives of biology, it may do so only to entrap us in what are often crueller imperatives of its own.'[2] Is war, then, merely an idea – a powerful but dangerous one that has inspired generations of young men foolishly to lay down their lives for what Wilfred Owen famously called 'some desperate glory'? As a Japanese proverb proclaims 'War is the art of embellishing death', but who is doing the embellishing? For most of history, poets have inspired many young men to go into battle. Today video games and war movies perform much the same function. If we were to tell ourselves a different story, then, could we finally eliminate war?

War is not an idea

On New Year's Day 2013 the artist Yoko Ono paid for a full-page advertisement in *The New York Times*. She then left it blank save for two words: 'Imagine Peace', an echo of John Lennon's most famous song. After it appeared, *The Guardian* conducted an opinion poll asking its readers whether the advertisement would promote world peace. Remarkably, a third of the respondents believed that it would, despite the murderous on-going civil war in Syria and the persistent conflict in Afghanistan. Wouldn't it be marvellous if war really were just an idea, a very bad one, and that the cause of peace could be achieved by merely imagining it? Haven't we been given an imagination by natural selection to escape from some of its imperatives? Even Richard Dawkins believes that we are not necessarily prisoners of our 'selfish genes'.

One writer to take this to heart is John Mueller, who has spent the past 30 years telling us that war is only an idea and that, like any idea, it may simply go out of fashion. War, he insists, is only an effect of the mind and somehow human beings have reasoned themselves into it over time. It follows that by an act of supreme imagination we can pull the plug. Slavery and duelling, two equally time-honoured institutions, eventually became obsolete after becoming unfashionable and then ridiculous. So why not war?[3]

Mueller's argument is provokingly superficial. It is meant to be deep but it is repeated so often that it soon begins to seem shallow. It is also made in the face of two inconvenient truths. The first is that slavery still persists. Indeed, there are more people in slavery now than at any time in human history. The campaigning organization Free the Slaves (FTS) estimates the number to be at least 27 million. And slavery is cheaper than ever. A slave in the 1850s at the time of Quentin Tarantino's film *Django Unchained* (2012) cost the equivalent of approximately $40,000 (in today's money). According to figures published by FST, the cost of a slave today averages around $90, depending on the work he or she is forced to carry out. In his book *McMafia* Misha Glenny tells the story of a young woman who was smuggled from Moldova to Cairo, then traded across the Sahara desert by Bedouins, before being sold in West Africa to Russians running a brothel in Tel Aviv, where she was forced to service 20 men a day. Unsurprisingly she became HIV positive.[4] This sex trafficking network is even more global than the Atlantic slave trade and all the more insidious because it is largely invisible. Slavery today is hidden behind many names, like bonded labour (which is most extensive in South Asia). And its reality has not changed at all in the intervening years: it is still about using others in whatever way serves another's interests, whether it is sex or child labour. Slaves are members of an out-group, and accordingly there is no moral constraint to feel their pain, or even sympathize with their plight.

The second inconvenient truth is that duelling is still with us in a different form. For the philosopher and jurist Lord Kames, writing in 1761, the 'darling principle' (as he called it) of all human nature was revenge. For Kames, the power of retribution was the motivating force of history, and as a good Enlightenment thinker he believed that the civilized thing to do was to transfer it from private to public hands. Gradually the law would become the only legitimate avenger. And once they surrendered personal recourse to the *lex talionis* (the law of retaliation) even duellists would become aware of civil society for the first time. They would become social beings as well as law-abiding ones. Kames even foresaw a time when people would no longer *want* to avenge themselves on those who wronged them. Tell that in the divorce courts in the United States with their 'Rambo litigation', or the law courts in London that do a profitable trade in 'libel tourism'. Both are excellent examples of the way in which duelling has moved from the field of honour to courts of law.

Mueller hardly helps his case by distracting lapses of plausibility, comparing slavery and duelling to other 'social evils' such as bear-baiting, bare-knuckle fighting and the burning of heretics. All of these are social practices, some of them quite old, some more recent (public cigarette smoking is the last on his list), but none of them are adaptive like slavery. And even then – and this is the point – slavery and duelling do not express our humanity or make us what we are; unlike war, they don't define our human nature, even though they exemplify nastier aspects of it.

And there is another, philosophical reason for questioning Mueller's thesis. As Jonathan Swift once remarked, you can't reason a person out of something that they weren't reasoned into. Take religion. A person believes in God either because it is part of a family belief system (ingested with mother's milk), or because of some personal epiphany (what the poet Czesław Miłosz calls 'an unveiling of reality'), or simply because it resonates – it is an emotional reality for the person concerned. Similarly, most people, if they give war any thought at all, would probably agree with the British strategist Basil

Liddell-Hart that 'war is always a matter of doing evil in the hope that some good may come of it'. If they think a little harder, they may even conclude that the democracies in which they are fortunate enough to live may be a product of war, and that sometimes we have to fight against evil whether we wish to or not.

War, Mueller insists, requires nothing to change, not human nature, or the international system, or the nation-state, or even our capacity for moral growth. As an idea, all we need is to *rethink* it, and we can do so without exporting democracy or prosperity, or reducing racism or nationalism. Most exponents of peace would profoundly disagree with him. They would contend that a person's moral consciousness is vitally important. Without a change in moral sensibilities it is unlikely that the Atlantic slave trade would have been abolished as early as it was. It only ended because enough individuals spoke out against it, and it is doubtful that individualism could have taken shape as decisively as it did until the novel had transformed the concept into narrative form.[5] Steven Pinker argues for that reason that we are what we read. 'The cliché that life imitates art is true because the function of some art is for life to imitate it.'[6] Although novels often embody ideas, it is the novel, not the idea, that is often more important in our cultural evolution. Or to put it another way, in this case the medium really is the message. Unless you grasp the way war is also promoted through what we read – and now watch on screen – you will be left always short of understanding. And we can't understand the modern mind without understanding the process of evolution; that is why evolutionary psychology arose in the first place. We are a story-telling species. Unless you grasp that war is not an 'idea' but a deeply ingrained cultural practice, you will be left crassly blaming its historical prevalence on the fact that our ancestors were too stupid to grasp its cost, or too naïve in thinking it 'glorious', or too blinkered to understand its consequences. We really need to think *through* war much more deeply than the 'endists' do with their very narrow focus on ideas, or economics, or technology. War is not one-dimensional. It is not just an idea, even if it is intensely ideational.

Cultural enhancement

In his book *Co-evolution: Genes, Culture, and Human Diversity* D.H. Durham argues that over thousands of years we have evolved to learn culture, in part because it helps us to adapt and live longer. The co-evolution model also assumes, however, that we will eventually 'breed' out maladaptive practices by selection against those who practise them – in the case of war those who derive their humanity from it: the warriors.[7] How would you 'select' against them? One way might be to challenge the hold they still have on our imagination thanks to the stories we still tell. Over the centuries they have been helped by what the contemporary philosopher Slavoj Žižek calls 'the military-poetic complex'. Taking the longer view, the novel is only one stage (the first was the epic poem) in the much longer history of the relationship between art and war. The focus of creative energy may have shifted to other manifestations of the relationship, in particular the film and video game, but the dynamic remains the same. Warriors are still popular for that reason; they enhance social life. The war game Call of Duty outsold every other form of entertainment in the UK in 2012 and has proved so popular that it now has its own social network.

War, in other words, is a *cultural enhancer*, Mark Pagel's term for anything that goes beyond mere survival and that exists solely to promote the interests of the replicant inside its vehicle. He takes the example of genetic enhancers (i.e., short strings of

DNA in our genomes that help genes function more effectively within their bodies or vehicles). Genes for growth need to be active early in life, and less so, or even not at all, later in life. They solve this problem by recruiting genetic enhancers that tell them when and where to be switched on and off. In turn, this makes it more likely the gene will survive and be passed on.[8]

The point about war is really the point about religion: both encourage us to believe in something. Without belief we would lead much less secure lives; we might also lead much diminished ones. It is easy to see how religion enhances the life of many believers (it gives them meaning, a source of consolation, especially in the presence of death). Religion reinforces psychological resilience, and thus makes communities stronger. The psychologist Kenneth Pargement has spent years looking at the links between religion and resilience, and attributes its power to its invocation of the sacred. And he has found that sacred coping mechanisms are still more effective than secular ones.[9] Richard Sosis has found the recitation of the Psalms among Israeli women helps them to deal with terrorist attacks.[10] It is another example of the nexus between war and religion which I discussed briefly in Chapter 1.

I think Iris Murdoch grasped this in her Gifford

lectures (*Metaphysics as a Guide to Morals*, 1992). God may not exist, but what led us to conceive of God does exist and is constantly experienced and pictured. Something similar seems to be true of war. Our prehistoric ancestors would sing before going into battle to enhance their courage. Pagel compares it to a performance-enhancing drug. It is a great cultural leap, of course, from fireside chanting to the epic poems of Homer, which inspired – and still do – generations of young soldiers. *The Iliad* privileges no culture, not even the language in which it was originally declaimed. Nearly three millennia later an English naval captain was inspired to quote a line from Alexander Pope's translation of the poem as he addressed the crew of his ship during the battle of Trafalgar (1805).[11] War has continued to enrich life, from the nineteenth-century novel (*War and Peace*, 1869) to the contemporary film (*Saving Private Ryan*, 1998). The case for art is not that it offers an escape from reality; on the contrary, it animates it. Our fictional heroes, like Achilles and Prince Andrei, are not larger than life; they are life's largeness, which is why we seek them out. War stories impart beliefs which still motivate many of us. They tell of heroic struggles against the out-group and supreme acts of sacrifice for the in-group, and only if they no longer continued to do so would we have reason to question whether war itself might be losing its 'iron grip' on life.

In fact, we spend a good deal of our lives locked in fictional worlds. And there is an evolutionary explanation for that, too. Stories have adaptive value: they teach us the basic social values and tend to encourage pro-social behaviour.[12] One recent Stanford University study found that video games, including violent ones, actively develop altruism and empathy in the players. In allowing some to become superheroes, they facilitate even greater pro-social behaviour (*The Times*, 31 January 2013). Through the medium of fiction, as Darwin insisted in *The Descent of Man* (1871), the warrior ideal allows us to escape from feelings of hopelessness and despair and so encourages us to face the worst with the strength of will to carry on. People are actually better because of the books they read and the video games they now play. As the cognitive psychologist Keith Oakley claims in *The Passionate Muse* (2012), we all want to be true to ourselves, and often we find that this can best be done by imagining what our fictional characters would have done in similar circumstances. Mimetic desire may seem absurd, of course, to those who don't buy into the Marvel comic myths, but for those who do it transfigures everyday life. Stories of heroism and sacrifice are still woven intrinsically into the fabric of human psychology.

This should not really surprise us. Although I make much in this short book of scientific hypotheses which tend to bracket off questions concerning whether there is value, meaning and intentional purpose present in what we do, this by no means implies the irrelevance of these questions. The nexus between religion and war is a remarkable one. Take sacrifice, which is the cornerstone of human altruism (which is not to be confused, of course, with co-operation: many effects of group living confer benefits – humans hunting together can kill larger prey; 'selfish genes' don't always produce selfish behaviour). But as we have evolved culturally, so we have produced altruistic behavioural patterns quite different from those of our primitive ancestors. In *The World until Yesterday*, Jared Diamond observes that the most critical difference in our own understanding of the psychology of war is the element of personal self-sacrifice, which is entirely absent. The very idea of never leaving a man down (so central to the ethos of units such as the US Marine Corps) would be completely alien to tribal thinking. At its worst, today's suicide bombers, like yesterday's Kamikaze pilots, can only be produced by societies that have been programmed from childhood to admire sacrifice for one's country or religious faith.[13]

Dying to be equal

In the end, discussion of the warrior as a human type brings us back to a very old debate between two of the most important philosophers of the modern era. Hegel agreed with Kant that war was 'something which ought to pass away', but he was not a member of what he called the 'peace party'. His real argument with Kant had less to do with the character of war than with its nature. Kant thought the elimination of war required moral progress. Hegel agreed that war was the manifestation of a specific moment in history and that its time would eventually pass, but not until it was no longer instantiated in human consciousness. War would continue, he contended, as long as there were people willing to fight for their principles and beliefs, and even sacrifice themselves for their ideas.[14]

Of course, by people he meant men. What is interesting about the future evolution of war, however, is that it is beginning to involve one half of the human species that traditionally has been excluded from the 'fraternity'. Women, too, may find war culturally enhancing. They already make up 15% of the US armed forces and have finally won the right to engage in combat in 2016. And although they have accounted since 9/11 for only 2% of casualties, 80% of female deaths in war zones have been categorized as 'hostile'. The female warrior has been a regular character in science fiction films and video games for some time, and has been a character in war too, not that the generals have always been willing to acknowledge it (the grunts have been more accepting). Today's wars no longer have fixed front lines – a female Marine driving a truck on the road to Kabul is as vulnerable as a male Marine on his second tour of duty in Helmand province; and women have been flying Apache helicopters into fire-fights and deploying deep into hostile territory as part of 'female engagement' teams despatched to talk to Afghan women. And all of this is happening at the very moment that the resilience of men in combat is coming into question as suicides outnumber battle casualties for the first time. If human nature has made men hunters and aggressors, certainly useful attributes in combat, those traits are also blamed for many of the mental problems soldiers now face: males now account for 95% of all suicides in the armed forces. Are women even mentally tougher than men? In a recent scientific study based on brain-scanning technology, neuroscientists found that women out-perform men in inductive reasoning and are better at keeping track of a fast-changing situation – in short, they get less stressed out (*The Sunday Times*, 3 March 2013).

The female warriors whom Plato first antici-pated in his great thought-experiment *The Republic* (Book 5) may be about to come into their own. It was Plato who wanted women to enter all aspects of public life, including war, on the grounds that biology takes its meaning from the values, customs and conventions of gender; that the differences between the two sexes and the relations they are deemed to *embody* are minor compared with the anatomical correspondences between the two. This development makes nonsense of the traditionalists' fear of the 'feminization' of war and some feminists' fear of the 'masculinization' of women. It is instead another striking example of how once again war is realizing another of its previously unrealized pos-sibilities.

Whether this is to be welcomed or not is largely beside the point. Cultural enhancement is like natu-ral selection. Both are colour-blind when it comes to morality. They promote what is most efficient. No-one, writes Pagel, would ask why armies in the

Middle Ages embraced longbows and later better guns and no-one today should wonder why we are allowing women to do combat. For some women, war – in Hegel's words – represents 'an existential choice: an assertion of will which defines the self and asserts its value'. Their numbers may be few, but they are likely to become contemporary heroes, just as some men have in the past, for courting danger and for the demanding and dangerous missions they are prepared to undertake. Even in the technologically defined discourse of war they will still represent human agency, battling against the odds and exercising their own discretion. And even if war were no longer to prove culturally enhancing it would not suddenly disappear. To return to Pagel's analogy of performance-enhancing drugs, 'those drugs might improve your performance in a foot race, but they are not the reason you are running'.[15]

3

Technology

'Our soldiers are warriors of character . . . our azimuth to the future.' So claimed General Schoomaker, the Chief of Staff of the US Army, in August 2003. An azimuth is the direction of a celestial object, an angular measurement of a spherical co-ordinate system, or so Wikipedia tells me. The technological azimuth to the future in the case of war around the turn of the twentieth century was not especially promising. Orville Wright later recalled that at the time he and his brother made their first manned flight in 1903, they believed that the invention of the aeroplane would bring an end to further wars. Marconi thought the coming of radio would make war 'ridiculous' (which was a variation on Oscar Wilde's claim that it would be repudiated only once it became vulgar, rather than wicked). My favourite example is that of Hiram Maxim, the inventor of the machine gun, who, when asked whether the invention would make war *more* wicked replied: 'No, it'll make war impossible.'

Although the technologies in question did not all promise a better or even safer world, nevertheless they each created more problems than they solved. Unfortunately, argues the great technology guru Kevin Kelly, problems are the answer to solutions.[1] As we have known for some time, once a machine is built, we soon discover that it has 'ideas' of its own. It changes not only our habits but also our habits of mind. The Maxim gun was a case in point. Far from making war impossible it allowed those who possessed it to occupy the moral high ground. Because only the West had it, contends John Ellis in *The Social History of the Machine Gun* (1993), it was deemed to be the product of a rational society. It followed that those who didn't have it (such as the Native Americans) were being irrational in continuing to resist the onward path of westward expansion. Inevitably, the Americans used it to make the natives 'see reason'; if they continued to resist, they were clearly being unreasonable. And, of course, it often worked. By 1890 the American frontier was officially closed and Geronimo, the last 'renegade' Indian leader, was finally captured. It was all to end badly for western societies, however.

Once they turned machine guns on each other they found themselves in a moral no-man's-land of their own making.

The question we should ask, writes Kelly, is this: What does technology still want of us? Let us be clear: technologies do not have needs or desires as we do. But when you add new technologies together they acquire a collective property, just as we talk of the market 'wanting' things (such as regulation, whether more or less, or new technologies for transferring wealth). And technological advances and insights often occur at about the same time in more than one place: the evolution of technology converges in much the same manner as biological evolution.

Kelly's imperative can also be seen as a variation of Richard Dawkins' influential idea of the extended phenotype. Dawkins tells us that birds and nests are one and the same. Without a nest (and the eggs they hold), birds could not reproduce themselves. Poorly constructed or poorly placed nests reduce a bird's chance for reproductive success. Conversely, well-built ones dramatically increase the evolutionary odds. Likewise, we are what technology makes us. No other species has such an extensive phenotype as we do. Technology is simply the further evolution of evolution; and technological evolution produces a variety of gadgets, machines, tools and techniques which help us to evolve its power to evolve. Moreover, the latest technologies, including the computer, are becoming smarter. They are offering new choices, not only in co-operation with us but for the first time in possible competition with us. They are making us more intelligent and more innovative at the very time that they may be about to develop an agenda of their own. Ray Kurtzweil calls it the Singularity – the day that computers become self-conscious (the Skynet scenario for those who are familiar with the *Terminator* franchise).

Until that day arrives – if ever – technology will continue to give us choices. Choices without values yield little, but new choices may also revalue or even devalue what traditionally we have held in high regard, such as sacrifice and heroism in the case of war. It is simply too soon to tell, although in my book *Warrior Geeks* (2013) I make the argument that this is precisely the direction in which technology is taking us. It is devaluing the sacramental ideal of war and persuading us to overvalue technical proficiency.

Specialization

One of the things that technology has always 'wanted' is increasing specialization. Evolution moves from the general to the specific. In primitive societies every adult male is a warrior; in state-centric societies professionals tend to come into their own. Specialization also extends to weapons, from the spear, which most people could throw, to the flint-lock musket and today's drones, which require specialist training.

And war has been becoming more specialized in another critical respect: human input is decreasing. Chemical power replaced muscle power a long time ago, around the fifteenth century, when longbows, which, with a draw weight of more than 100 lb, required considerable physical strength, were abandoned in favour of muskets. (Even the Brown Bess rifles used at Waterloo, however, were less accurate and lethal than bow technology. If the Redcoats had been armed with longbows the battle would have been an easy 'away' win rather than a 'damned close-run thing', as the Duke of Wellington actually admitted.) The physical labour of war has been diminishing for some time now and will be reduced further still; even the 'grunts' will have their strength enhanced by exoskeletons and, possibly, performance-enhancing drugs. As Kelly claims, specialization domesticates us; and at the cutting edge war continues to demand what Mark Pagel calls 'a more domesticated set of abilities'. By 'domesticated' both writers mean more cerebral. The 'analytical warrior' is in the process of replacing the stereotypes of old. Mental agility, communication skills and multi-tasking will be the virtues required of tomorrow's warriors. Culture has still not stopped sorting out our talents, and many of us (including women) will continue to have a talent for war.[2]

What is really powering the move towards ever-increased specialization is the digital age, another illustration of how our evolution and technology have been running along parallel lines for some time. Both are born in generality and grow to specificity; what is unique to us as a species is the interplay between our genes pushing us towards a particular outcome, and our cultures producing technologies that respond to our talents. This constantly tends to shift the goalposts of our existence, though shifting must fit what we are disposed to want to do, and what we are still capable of doing. And we are still predisposed, I would argue, to engage in war, and just as capable of waging it, and soon in completely new dimensions.

Technology

'A short-sighted vulgarity'

'The next war will be in cyberspace' are the unambiguous words of General Keith Alexander, the first head of the US Cyber-Command. As cyberspace becomes the next battle space, a new arms race may already be underway. The 15 countries with the biggest military budgets are investing in offensive cyber-capabilities and are still figuring out how to integrate cyberwarfare capabilities into military operations. Even if we are not yet militarizing cyberspace, wittingly or unwittingly we are militarizing the idea.[3] We have already seen cyber-attacks on three countries (Iran, Estonia, Georgia), and they will not be the last. We now face all manner of cyber-prefixed threats, from 'cyber-espionage' to 'cyber-terror' and even 'cyber-geddon', and these, in turn, have engendered other cyber-prefixed neologisms, such as 'cyber-security', 'cyber-power' and 'cyber-strategy'.

Cyberwar itself, however, may be some way off. An act of war must be instrumental, political and potentially lethal. In this respect, the cyber-attacks we have witnessed so far have failed to make the cut. In the cyberworld it is 1929 – we are still in the age of dirigibles and biplanes. But we are transiting into the future faster than we think. In principle, it may be possible to shut down a whole city (urbicide is the term of art). Power grids could be sabotaged and air traffic control systems unplugged. Although it is far from clear whether the same dynamics that govern the use of conventional weapons will apply in cyberspace, we do know that cyber-weapons will become more complex, especially when computer viruses begin to learn. A virus that could 'learn' would be able to assess its environment and then act autonomously, and if programmed with evolutionary algorithms, it could 'evolve' in ways its original designers could not possibly predict.

Cyberwarfare, however, is only part of that larger cybernetic world in which we are locking the warriors of tomorrow. Science fiction has anticipated this for some time. Take Orson Scott Card's *Ender's Game* (1985), a novel which is on the syllabus of the Marine Corps University at Quantico. It is about a young cadet who takes part in a simulated battle sequence against an alien species called the Formics, only to discover at the end of the book that the battle is not a game; it is for real. There is a sobering remark halfway through the novel: 'Ender Wiggins isn't a killer. He just wins – *thoroughly*.' And this is the main challenge. Wiggins is a striking example of what the poet T.S. Eliot, in a very different context, called the 'dissociation of sensibility'.

He was arguing that before the modern age poets were able to express their thoughts through the experience of feeling; afterwards, they failed to unite their thoughts with their emotional experiences and instead expressed thought separately from feeling, and were the lesser poets for it. The issue with digital technology is that it requires a high degree of imagination. Most of us will continue to live in a world determined by physical proximity and presence. We will continue to see the immediate consequences of our actions with our own eyes. Cyberwarriors, by contrast, will have to apprehend in the mind what is objectively real; for them reality will only be intelligible purely through cognition. And this may become problematic if their social intelligence is found wanting, especially if they are unable to empathize with the enemies they are being asked to 'take out'.

This may appear counter-intuitive but it is really not. Our minds from very early on in our prehistory have fostered social intelligence. The psychologist Nicholas Humphrey describes cultivating plants as a 'conversation' similar to a mother talking to a two-month-old child: both are attuned respectively to a plant's or child's 'emergent properties'. Many of our most prized technological discourses, he surmises, from agriculture to chemistry, may have had their origins in the fortunate misapplication of social intelligence.[4] In other words, we are pro-social beings that build up relationships with 'others', whether animate or inanimate. In privileging the specialized cognitive domain of technical intelligence, however, we may already be moving into a less socially intelligent world, one in which warriors may become more self-absorbed and certainly more self-regarding. Neuroscientists tell us that the primitive pain centre in the brain activates almost immediately when pain is recalled but the ability to empathize with the prolonged suffering of others unfolds more slowly; it takes time to understand the moral dimension of a situation, and this is largely communicated though reflection. Dissociation, in other words, is not just an attitude of mind; it is a function of changes in the brain, and the digital world may already be beginning to change the architecture of the human brain itself and, therefore, what it means to be human.[5]

A striking example of the direction in which we may be going is offered by an article in *The Economist* entitled 'Battle Ready', with its radical conclusion that 'it may be necessary to vaccinate our soldiers against the trauma of war' (*The Economist*, 17 November 2012). This might be possible, it argued, if scientists could eliminate the conflicting emotions and challenges that have characterized war throughout history, denying soldiers as a result some of its remaining existential rewards. None of this is entirely unanticipated. Writing back in 1952, Isaiah Berlin warned that cybernetics (not the atomic bomb) marked the most disturbing change in the character of war. In the cybernetic battle spaces of the future, servicemen would feel and think quite differently. 'This is what marks a real change,' he argued, 'and all the talk about "the atomic age" is a kind of short-sighted vulgarity.'[6] He may well be proved right.

War by algebra

We are human only to the extent that others recognize their humanity in us. Well, that is the story that western societies have been telling themselves for some time, but it may be difficult to persist with it when soldiers and robots start sharing the battle space together. In June 2006 the first armed and remote controlled robots in the history of warfare were deployed in Baghdad. As technology develops, robots will take many forms. Only excessive anthropomorphism encourages us to think they will look like the machines in the *Terminator* films.

With the development of nanotechnology some may swarm. Other smaller robots with sensors will be able to 'map' an entire city before the heavy-duty robots move in, seamlessly merging automated surveillance with automated killing. Some roboticists are even looking at the humble amoeba for inspiration. Quite stiff when compressed, robots may be able to flow like liquids when given room, thus allowing them to enter any space no smaller than their compressed state, more or less regardless of the shape of the area in question.

'Killer robots' are undoubtedly coming our way, but not all robots will be armed, and not all armed robots will be without 'humanity', the name we give not only to a species but also to the qualities we deem it to embody. Unlike most other technologies, from the machine gun to the submarine, whose inventors thought them so terrible that they would bring war to an end, no-one has made the same claim for robots, although a number of critics, such as Human Rights Watch, have urged they be banned before it is too late. The Bureau of Investigative Journalism has even described the use of drones as a form of 'industrialized killing'. Nothing, in fact, could be further from the truth. What is happening is part of a historical cycle, the attempt to make war more humane. Some weapons are even deemed to have a 'moral character' because they allow us to be more discriminating in our targeting. And since 2007 the US military has been trying to program the next generation of machines with a 'conscience' (a set of computer algorithms in place of the moral heuristics that are hard-wired into us by natural selection).

In the not too distant future robots may be able to evaluate the consequences of their own actions. Indeed, the ability to reach value judgements will be part of their program. The fact that empathy and compassion will be beyond their 'emotional range' will hardly matter since both will be 'offset' – so we are told – by what should really count: consistency of behaviour. Robots won't have prejudices, personal or generic, and they won't misbehave under stress. The reduction of inhumanity will 'offset' the loss of humanity; the result may be a fighting force that is more humane than an all-human one.[7] 'I will stand my artificial intelligence over your humanity any day of the week,' a key American military commentator remarked recently, 'and tell you that my AI will . . . create fewer ethical lapses than a human being.'[8]

Robots, in other words, could radically change the face of war. They would negate the need for courage and hatred (two of the 'moral factors' which Clausewitz held to be central to the nature of war since our remote ancestors first sat by their camp fires and sang their war songs on the eve of battle). Hatred is the projection of our own identity onto others who are deemed to threaten it, or who (at best) are just deemed to be 'different'. Because robots would never hate anyone they would act more humanely on our behalf (a telling commentary on our lack of belief in our own humanity). Even John Gray, who questions whether we have any real agency, concedes that we don't always have to make a choice. But such a human being, he adds, would have the perfect freedom of a machine (programed to do someone else's bidding).[9] And there's the rub. Instead of offering an environment in which moral conundrums are constantly tested and debated, war would deprive the soldier of any responsibility for his or her actions. Soldiers would rely on algorithmic gatekeepers (a computer program). They would rely on machines to 'automate' human virtue.

I suspect that the real game changer is what technology may still want of us. Robots may eventually enable us to replace human rationality with *logic* – cold, calculating and utterly relentless, like the Categorical Imperatives of Immanuel Kant (which are instantiated in Asimov's 3 Laws of Robotics). It was Kant who told us that we should never lie.

If we offer a friend refuge from the police, we are obliged, if asked, to tell them where he is hiding, even though most of us might think it would be morally impermissible to do so. In real life we are not consistent; even the state is sometimes willing to suspend the law so that justice can be better served. Even scientists suspect logical reasoning. As the nuclear physicist Niels Bohr once rebuked a student: 'Stop being so bloody logical, and start thinking.'

If this is indeed the direction in which we are heading, it would have surprised Clausewitz, and even appalled him. In his great work *On War* he argued that it was a 'fallacy to conceive of war as ridding itself of human passion. The result, if one could, would be war by algebra.'[10] But that is what may be on the horizon, and it should give us a cause for concern – not because robots will be unable to perform the tasks we give them, but because war is not algorithmic. Many experts are worried that, once we arm robots, they may turn their weapons on us. But the real challenge we face may be very different: should we really abdicate responsibility for our actions to machines, however sophisticated? Merely to think in such terms inevitably raises a rather disturbing question: not whether war is bad for us, but whether we are bad for war.

Technology

Is war getting smaller?

Even more pertinent than the age-old question 'How long will we fight wars?', the future prompts us to ask another question: 'How long will war still need us?' Doubtless on the battlefields of tomorrow soldier and machine will co-exist in an uneasy relationship, but there can be little doubt that the scientists will continue to reduce the human space of war still further. I am reminded of the film *Sunset Boulevard* (1950), in which the journalist Joe Gillis says to the former star Norma Desmond: 'You used to be in silent pictures; you used to be big.' To which she replies: 'I *am* big; it's the pictures that got small.'

Like the pictures, the future is shrinking, claims Danny Hillis, one of the founders of the Long Now Foundation. This may be because we have handed it over to the geeks and their gadgets.[11] It would be pretty pointless, I fear, to complain about this development. The future belongs to the more cerebral warrior, wired into a networked world. Today the weapon of choice is the drone (the US has 20,000 of them) and the model warrior the drone pilot, for whom there is now a new decoration, the Distinguished Warfare Medal, which, until the Pentagon eventually yielded to protests from within the military, was deemed to be more important than either the Bronze Star or the Purple Heart.

If this is indeed the future, fiction writers have been engaging with it for some time. In his 1997 novel *Towards the End of Time*, John Updike imagined a war between China and the United States in 2020. Looking back at a 'dwindled world', his anguished hero regrets that the war had been run by 'highly trained young men and women in sealed chambers of safety reading 3-D computer graphics'.[12] Sometimes, of course, truths that may grow laboured in a novel are more deftly evoked in a short story, and a favourite example of mine is Don DeLillo's 'Human Moments in World War III' (1983), the tale of a young twenty-first century pilot, Vollmer, in an orbital space station, a new breed of cerebral warrior: 'an engineering genius, a communications and weapons genius', a veritable postmodern warrior with degrees in science and technology. The moral of the tale lies not in the text but in the sub-text. War exists only on the margins of Vollmer's consciousness; it has become a 'routine', a series of housekeeping arrangements. War takes place at a firing panel where Vollmer can wear his carpet slippers and a football jersey bearing the number 79, 'a prime of no particular distinction'. At one point in the story he tells his commanding officer that he is happy, only to be reminded that happiness is not one of the 'mission parameters'. The world, we gather from the story, has grown smaller and war with it, which is why Vollmer's gaze seems to be cast backwards at his own vacancy.

The world is just as large as ever, of course; it is war that is getting smaller. Unfortunately, that does not portend its end. We tend to think of our minds these days as computers – absorbing data, processing them and making our bodies perform the output; we often conceive of our bodies as hardware and minds as software. But the mind doesn't just accumulate information, it thinks; it creates; it imagines – and there's the rub. Imagination can be creative but it can also be dysfunctional; sometimes we imagine unreal fears and insults and we behave unpredictably as a result. Militaries since the time of Descartes have tried to make soldiers 'cheerful robots' for that reason – to program the way they behave through operational analysis, for example, or systems engineering in the recent past. In the near future they may finally succeed. Vollmer may be an avatar of the shape of things to come. Indeed, what I suspect we may be witnessing is only the end of the beginning: the story of war as a purely human activity (what Thucydides called 'the human thing'). And it is a little too early to judge whether the first phase is about to end and the next to begin.

4

Geopolitics

Wars are not only generated by cultural and technological developments; they are also generated by storytelling. No matter how hard we strive for purely rational thought there will always be narratives that lend our consciousness a specifically human meaning. There is a deep yearning in the human psyche to be rooted in a 'story' such as that of the imagined community (the nation). Storytelling often makes us less fearful; often, however, it may make us more. It can make us too imaginative; it may be a trivial epiphenomenon of our evolutionary fitness, not a survival mechanism at all. And yet it is the narratives that we construct that give history its shape and meaning, and it is only through these narratives that history occurs. History renews its energy from the stories we tell.[1]

Since the world first went global in its own

imagination – around the 1890s – we have been telling ourselves geopolitical tales, and one of the predominant discourses today is globalization. If the global is the sum of multiple local activities with worldwide range, consequences and significance, globalization involves the interpenetration of these activities. And it is the degree of interpenetration – or so we are told – that makes it increasingly difficult to imagine that any major power would contemplate war against another. Yet, as always, this attractive vision, even if true, comes at a price. For the many critics of globalization, from Joseph Stieglitz to Masao Miyoshi, more and more of the world's people are being integrated into a geopolitical system that denies all but the most powerful a voice in their own future.

The state, market and international order

The contention that globalization is making war less attractive is certainly popular. David Held and Anthony McGrew contend that all countries today are engaged in international trade (around 20% of world output is now traded). And if, in the past, trade sometimes was quarantined off from the main economy, it is now an integral part of the structure of national production in all modern states. As a result, national markets have become increasingly inter-connected. All states are now enmeshed in what they call a 'world military order'. And Held and McGrew conceive what they call 'military globalization' as a process which is producing 'structural bifurcation': that is, fragmentation into two largely separate systems, each with different standards and rules of conduct. The costs of a conventional, let alone nuclear, war are now so great that major war has become obsolete. 'It would be counter-productive, either as a mechanism for resolving inter-state conflict, or as a mechanism for transforming the international status quo. In distinction to this, states on the periphery (the developing world) operate in a system . . . in which there is no effective deterrent to war.'[2]

This argument is not new. Back in the nineteenth century Cobden and Bright were among the first to argue that trade, not war, was a more effective generator of national wealth. A little later, in his book *The Great Illusion* (1909), Norman Angell argued that war between great powers, at least, had become zero-sum. In any future conflict the victors would suffer as much as the vanquished. Even Herbert Spencer (the father of Social Darwinism) spotted the declining economic value of antipathy when he wrote in the 1870s that war had given all it had to give. 'No further benefits could be looked for from it.'[3] In other words it had become maladaptive; it no longer paid dividends on belief.

The Great Illusion was published a few years before the outbreak of the First World War and it came to define an entire generation of writers who felt that if only their message had resonated more loudly the world would have been spared the conflict. But we tend to forget what Angell was actually saying, because few of his apologists bother to read his book. It is not quite the peace tract that its exponents think it is. Angell took ideas seriously, and that, in part, was the problem. They were *his* ideas (or rather they were the commonplace thoughts of his compatriots). The real conflict, Angell insisted – as though it were self-evident, was not between Germany and England, but between democracy and autocracy, socialism and individualism, and especially reaction and progress, 'however one's sociological sympathies may classify them'.

This was the problem. The classifications were all-important and Angell's sympathies were never in doubt for a moment. He took it as a given that his own country was the guarantor of 'the operation of free economic forces', and that 'the extension of the dominating principle of the British Empire to European society as a whole is the solution of the international problem which this book argues'. *The Great Illusion*, in other words, was a liberal-imperialist manifesto directed at German opinion. It was not a classic economic text concerned with free market principles.[4]

'Politics is the new economics,' an international banker remarked recently (*The Times*, 31 January 2013), but it has ever been the case. He was referring to the fact that at the heart of the Eurozone's present travails are fundamental questions about how far Europe's integration can be taken by way of pooling its debt. But behind all economic theories are philosophies of how markets work, or should do, and how people behave, or should be encouraged to behave. Ideas matter, and the story of the outbreak of war in 1914 is that of the collapse of an entire system of thought – the progressive weakening of liberal thinking in Germany, the rise of a social Darwinian zero-sum competitive idea of economics, coupled with a disdain for economics itself. The enthusiasm with which Europe's youth went to war was partly the manifestation of a collective ennui produced by the long peace.

One of the problems with today's 'democratic capitalism' (to invoke Michael Novak's term) is that the market is only as resilient as the ideas that sustain it. And those ideas in the 2008 financial crisis proved very thin. We find ourselves living in an ideological vacuum which is unlikely to persist much longer between a growing disenchantment with socialism and unsustainable welfare spending, and a profound distrust of the power of market capitalism to continue generating wealth. In many western countries, 25% of today's youth will be less wealthy than the previous generation – a challenge the world has not had to face for some time. And the decline of community life – in Francis Fukuyama's dismal vision of the future *The End of History and the Last Man* (1992) – could lead either to even greater self-absorption (a kind of nihilistic narcissism), or bloody, if pointless, prestige battles, only this time fought with modern weapons.

Another reason for invoking Angell is that he did not realize that the territorial states of his day (lumbered with their huge empires) were inevitably on a collision course. Imperialism might not be the 'highest stage of capitalism' (as Lenin contended), but territorial states were distinctly different from the trading states of today. Richard Rosencrance has argued for some time that great powers now use trade to acquire the raw materials that they once tried to secure by military force. As a result, they have prospered and found little incentive to wage war. Trading states do not need to control territory and its resources. They enrich themselves by developing international commercial networks; and if they still compete with each other, they do so not for territory but for market share. Accordingly, Rosencrance contends, the main trend in international politics in the past half-century has been against the very notion of another great power conflict.[5]

Yet it is by no means certain that territory will not become important once again. We simply don't know what is going to happen with climate change and the natural resources it may 'unlock' for exploitation. And as other resources become scarce (such as fresh water), so territoriality might once more gain significance and the scope for war increase as a result. The competition for resources between the world's leading economies may also make *access* to territory (rather than formal control) more important than ever. Between 2006 and 2013 China invested almost $500 billion across the globe, three-quarters of it in the developing world, to secure the raw materials that its voracious economic expansion urgently needs. The authors of one recent book talk of 'a slow but steady conquest' of the developing world by China in collusion with local elites – a process they call globalization of the many for the few. The point is not that western companies are also not exploitative but that the collusion between Chinese companies and local elites may 'lock out' other countries and make it more, not less likely, that countries will engage in 'resource wars'.[6]

Ultimately, however, the whole argument against the profitability of war ignores the fundamental connection between war and the state which was so memorably formulated by Charles Tilly: 'war makes the state and the state makes war'. The relationship is a symbiotic one. Philip Bobbitt has taken this thesis further into the future.[7] War and the state, he argues, have always co-existed, and will continue to do so, in a mutually affecting relationship. Fundamental innovations in war bring about fundamental transformations in the constitutional structure of states, which, in turn, bring about fundamental changes in the conduct of war. The very changes in social complexity that it engineers feed back into the way it is conducted.

What has occurred most recently is that nation-states have become market-states, and Bobbitt is at pains to remind his readers that the latter are not uniform in character but take many forms. Entrepreneurial market-states tend to have as little government intervention as possible, maximizing opportunities through market mechanisms.

Mercantile market-states have a strong central government to protect national industries, taking a more directive role in determining areas of economic growth. Managerial market-states seek free open markets within regional trading networks, as well as applying stringent monetary policies.

And it is striking that market-states are still as much in the war business as the nation-states of the last century. With their emphasis on efficiency and economy they demand that the military act within tight budgets, accept fewer casualties and not involve themselves in potentially ruinous hostilities.[8] Market-states are, to that extent, war-averse, but they are not averse to employing war to secure their own interests, or maximize commercial opportunities. And one day, writes one Pentagon-watcher, the market-state military may even adapt the market-driven dynamics of companies like eBay. A commanding general might post tactical objectives on a website and assign values to them: 100 points for capturing a bridge; 500 for capturing a town. Various units could log on to see what is listed and 'bid' for whatever is there, making war itself in the process self-synchronizing, more adaptive and more effective.[9] Of course, this is to take current developments to their logical conclusion and, as we know, history is never logical, which is why it is impossible to make predictions by extrapolating current trends into the future. But what is happening already is no less suggestive in what it reveals about the evolving character of war. The US military now outsources not only its research to the civilian sector, but also the loading of systems like Predator drones to private contractors. Both are a form of 'crowd sourcing' – harvesting the collective wisdom of the community to obtain better results.

The new geopolitical thinking

Geopolitics as we know the term really only dates back to the late nineteenth century and it continues to have certain ground rules. Firstly, there is usually an enemy and its identity is not important for the cogency of the theory itself. What is important is that competition should be the motivating force in international affairs. Secondly, geopolitics also assumes a 'reading' of geography (maps) which is often over-deterministic, even fatalistic. Finally, it assumes a permanent interest: the balance of power as countries rise and others wane. To make sense of the strategic history there must also be a major conceptual framework: usually the prevailing political

order, which is often fragile and in need of buttress-
ing (often by military force).

Critical geopolitics emerged in the 1990s in
opposition to what was thought to be the crude
geographic determinism that lay behind some of
the century's most violent conflicts. Its claim is not
an unreasonable one: it is only the transposition of
the political onto geographical realities that allows
those realities to assume an often spurious geopolitical significance. Its agenda is usually radical
or left-inspired, and its exponents certainly reject
much of the thinking underlying the Global War
on Terror (GWOT), including its narratives of fear.
For them geography is 'space', which they claim
to be a social construction. We are what we think
ourselves to be, not passive victims of geographical
determinism. Land powers and sea powers are not
fated to find each other in conflict; even the identity
of 'core' and 'periphery,' or 'North and South',
is what we make of it. As the great literary critic
Northrop Frye argued in *Fearful Symmetry*, '[T]he
centre of reality is wherever one happens to be, and
its circumference is whatever one's own imagination can make sense of.'[10] Unfortunately, politicians
aren't literary critics and few governments tell
themselves such stories. China and Russia, like the
United States, don't 'talk back' to geopolitics; they

still talk geopolitics, and as long as they continue to do so war will be a possibility, powered by what has always given it its form: the narratives we tell.

But the geopolitical imagination is continuing to evolve. Critical geopolitics is evidence of this – it is both a continuation of and a radical break with what has gone before; it is simultaneously critical and complicit. It discourages us from seeing maps, as we once did, as the spatial representations of humanity's divisions, whether real or imagined, and no less real, of course, for merely being imagined. But it also encourages us to map emotions and desires. One such book is Robert Kaplan's *The Revenge of Geography*, which talks of the rise of a new discipline, *sociography*, to help us grasp 'a new urban geography of intense personal longing in the megacities of tomorrow (vast citadels of solitary striving)'.[11] And our maps of such longing may soon be as detailed as the depictions of the cities themselves.

Another work concerned with the emotional landscape is Dominique Moisi's *The Geopolitics of Emotions*, in which he divides the world into three groups. The first are the countries of hope, such as China and India, which are striving to catch up with the West and even overtake it. They are interested in economic growth, not in the management of global affairs. They express little interest, for example, in whether countries like Iran become nuclear powers, although they are becoming interested in the environment because climate change has economic consequences. The second group includes countries that feel humiliated by history. Many of them are to be found in the Islamic world: they are resentful about their public powerlessness and private misery, which they tend to blame on the West. But they also number Putin's Russia, no longer a superpower but a superannuated, angry country. And then there is the West, which is fearful of the future – fearful of the countries of appetite because they are in the process of out-producing and overtaking it; and also fearful of the countries of resentment because they tend to export terrorism.[12]

If we look at the world in these terms there is very little reason to think that we can avoid conflict. Take the countries of resentment. What would happen if Iran were to acquire nuclear weapons and other Middle East powers were to follow suit? Like John Mueller, one might argue that nuclear weapons simply don't matter, or, like Kenneth Waltz, one might argue that they are all that matter; a multinuclear world would be a much safer place than it is today. It may also be true that a 'nuclear taboo' has become established among nuclear powers just as there is an incest taboo in all cultures because of the realization that endogamy gives negative results. But such taboos don't arise overnight and both Russia and the US are still geared towards a hair-trigger response to launch their missiles against each other, even though neither threatens the other, ideologically or politically.

But it is the prospect of a poly-nuclear Middle East that not only the West but also Israel find frightening because, rightly or not, they suspect that the rules that helped to sustain the nuclear balance between the superpowers will not hold. A nuclear arms race in the region will make it more likely that weapons will fall into the hands of non-state actors, such as Hizballah. The role of religion in political decision-making also raises questions of rationality. Indeed, the real challenge may be *emotional*. The two superpowers were largely *status quo*. They carved out their own spheres of influence. They never trusted each other completely, but they had no ideological or political rationale to eliminate the other. The history of sectarian violence in the Arab world would suggest that religion is no obstacle to nuclear war. Indeed, the apocalyptic nature of religion itself suggests quite the opposite. Most disturbing of all, writes Ron Rosenbaum, is our apocalyptic thinking. Deep down, we really may be a species obsessed with its own self-destruction, 'obsessively scripting fiery self-immolations, cataclysmic conclusions to the human saga'.[13]

A *multiplicity of spaces*

We are constantly reinterpreting our world, in part because it is so much more varied and diverse than it used to be – or, rather, since it is we who have changed and not it, than the one we thought we once knew so well. We are beginning to realize, for example, that space too is a relative term; we are always creating new spaces of political action in which conflict can breed. One such space is actually its absence, a nice Derridean paradox. It is to be found in the part of the world that numbers the 1 billion poorest people on the planet living on less than $1 a day, as well as those who inhabit the *non-places* of our world, the ghastly ghettoes and sink estates of our own cities. Thus, writes the French anthropologist Marc Augé, we can contrast the realities of transit (transit camps or passengers in transit) with those of residence or dwelling; the interchange (where nobody crosses anyone else's path) with the crossroads (where people meet); the housing estate where people live separate lives with the gated community where they huddle together in fear of everyone else.[14] I see no sign of these non-spaces disappearing any time soon, which is why we must assume history will continue along the old lines, sparing us none of the bloody resolutions to come.

Then there is cyberspace, which many people once believed naïvely would make for a more humane world. The Internet, we were told, did not carry the baggage of history. The next generation would be liberated from the limitations of geographical proximity as the sole basis of friendship, collaboration and even neighbourhood. And if identity is geography and both are destiny, then the Net's de-spatialization of interaction promised a more harmonious world. Cyberspace, one of the co-founders of the Net-Wise Global Business Network even claimed, would reduce nationalism to the strength and relative weight of brand loyalty, like a fan's relationship to his local football team.[15]

Today, we are much less naïve than we once were, for we have discovered that the essence of cyberspace is not its material connections but its logical ones. It breeds communities like Al-Qaeda. And any community that shares a 'world' is necessarily bound into a network of responsibilities. Cyberspace is an 'infinite cage' which can imprison people in their present identities and nationalist logos. Sometimes, it may even rob them even of the desire to break out. The cyberspaces we inhabit are articulated by communities of people who cannot express their ideas about reality except through the medium of language, and one of the languages we speak is that of religion, which has given rise to conflict from the very beginning of the human story.

And then there is outer space. We have already been using space for military purposes for some time – we depend on satellites for reconnaissance (optical/infrared), electronic intelligence gathering and missile early warning systems. Space has been effectively militarized since the 1960s. The only difference is that we have not put weapons in orbit yet. Doing so would be as large a change as the opening of the air in 1903, for classical geopolitical thinking may hold in outer space as it does on earth, even if it will be open to modification. Everett Dolman, one of the leading space war theorists, predicts an astropolitical future, and he formulates a timely (and rather disturbing) astropolitical dictum: 'Who controls Low-Earth orbit controls Near-Earth space. Who controls Near-Earth space dominates the Terra. Who dominates Terra determines the destiny of humankind.'[16] For space strategies are unlikely to differ much from one of the oldest forms of naval warfare: the blockade.

Blockading could involve obstructing space communications by interfering with uplinks, downlinks and crosslinks. Whatever form of interference is chosen, the desired outcome would be to prevent the enemy from using celestial lines of communication. The point is that a space arms race is not only inevitable, it has probably already begun. An *astropolitical* arms race could propel either the US or China to try to seize control of Low-Earth orbit.

In short, one of the things we took for granted in geopolitics – the separation between earth and space – is coming to an end. The very word 'geopolitics', with its origins in the Greek word for 'earth', refers to our planet and nothing else. Such distinctions may soon collapse together with many others, such as those demarcating the finite and infinite and necessity (earth-bound) and freedom (the limitlessness of space). So many of the terms that constitute the language of warfare may well disappear, in the process investing its actual practice with renewed significance.

Great power war?

Let us return to the prospect of great power war. Is a war between the US and China really inconceivable, or for that matter between the US and Russia, or India and China (the last conflict they fought was in 1962)? Much will depend on the future of the present world order. In a recent book, *War, Religion and Empire* (2011), Andrew Phillips discusses three such orders: Latin Christendom before Westphalia; the Sinosphere, which was already 700 years old when European warships first arrived in the South China Seas; and finally the present post-1945 order. What makes his study interesting is the importance he attaches to the role of war in both underpinning and undermining all international orders, past and present.

Thus in sixteenth-century Europe the old order was destroyed by the Reformation, which polarized Christendom between a Protestant north and Catholic south, and the gunpowder revolution, which transformed war and made it more lethal. Likewise in East Asia the Sinosphere – the Chinese tribute system – was destroyed from inside by rebellion and from without by the European powers which had industrialized warfare and overtaken the country which had invented gunpowder. Every international order, Phillips also reminds us, is normative. It is underpinned by a value system; it is underwritten by ideas of how the world *should* work. In the case of Latin Christendom the

Reformation destroyed the Augustinian political order that had observed a delicate balance between the secular and the spiritual, between the kingship of states and the claims of the Papacy. In the course of the nineteenth century the Europeans also imposed a new normative order on the Chinese, who were forced at gunpoint into a system that was both contractual (based as it was on international law) and egalitarian (in theory, at least, all sovereign natures were equal in the eyes of international lawyers, even if some were more equal than others).

The stability of the present international system will depend on whether China is able to escape the fate of becoming late nineteenth-century Germany and avoid finding itself on a collision course with the US. But it will also depend on the ability of the world's two greatest powers to deal with the subversive element, especially religious fundamentalism. They were united in their response to 9/11, but the consensus they achieved is fragile. They still cannot agree on what punishment to mete out to transgressors such as North Korea, or how best to deter future transgressors like Iran from getting nuclear weapons. Phillips himself remains convinced of two inescapable imperatives. Because all orders are normative (because they embody distinct visions of the good), they will always be susceptible to subversion by groups like Al-Qaeda, and because they are fragile, we will have to be ready to defend them by the collective violence we call 'war'.

5

Peace

The closing years of the twentieth century saw a host of books with titles such as Charles McKibben's *The End of Nature* (1990) and John Horgan's *The End of Science* (2012). Most famous of all, perhaps, was Francis Fukuyama's *The End of History* (1992). I never thought we should see a book called *The End of War*, but Horgan wrote one in 2012; it also happens to be extremely unconvincing.

Not that there are no examples in history of societies which have not gone out of the war business – debellicized is the term used by historians and political scientists. My favourite is Sweden, once one of the most feared military powers in Europe. When in the 1820s the Swedish parliament debated whether to plant more oak trees, so that the all-wooden navy would be suitably resourced in a hundred years' time, the country was already out of the war business, had it but known it (its last war was against Russia in 1809). But the ability to do so is dependent entirely on the security offered by the international system. And the present international order is a fragmented one, with market-states jostling with old-fashioned nation-states like Russia and China. In addition, 33 countries currently carry the designation of 'fragile states' (20 of them in Africa). The post-Cold War rash of civil wars and imploding polities such as Somalia and Yugoslavia may have gone for now, but violence still prevails in large parts of the globe.

So what are the chances of getting the international community to eliminate war? 'Choosing Peace' is one of the chapter headings of Horgan's book. One way of doing so would be to legislate against war, but even Horgan admits that this prospect is not very realistic, and he is forced back, as are so many 'endists', onto a pious hope in the efficacy of non-violent action. It is a hope that does not inspire much confidence given the disappointing outcome of the Arab Spring, where nearly 100,000 people have died so far in Syria alone. The list of victims is already long and unfortunately set to lengthen.

The main reason that Horgan and Mueller and others like them are so unconvincing in their arguments is that they tend to dichotomize war and peace, and, as Aristotle told us in *The Politics*, this is quite impossible. The only purpose of war, after all, he wrote, is peace, however we choose to define it. Aristotle was the first philosopher to raise the question: what does it profit a state to win a war only to lose the peace that follows it? That is why any satisfactory theory of peace must also involve a theory of war.

Kant's wager

Immanuel Kant's essay *Towards Perpetual Peace* (1795) was the first ever penned on how to achieve it and it was a good deal more modest than many subsequent academic scribblings on the same theme. Indeed, he prefaced his essay with what he called a 'saving clause' in which he pointed out that his opinions were those of a mere 'theoretical politician', and that 'worldly-wise statesmen' were under no obligation to heed them (which is just as well, as most haven't).

Kant's contribution was to accept that the state of war was natural (here he took issue with writers such as Rousseau), and that peace would have to be grounded in human institutions. He is famous for discussing three: republican governments (his word for democracy); the idea of a federation of free states, an embryonic United Nations; and a concept of world citizenship (which gelled with the Enlightenment belief in the unity of humanity).

There are so many problems with Kant's enterprise it is difficult to know where to begin, and in a book as short as this I have to be brief. To be sure, multilateralism has changed the rules of the game. Beginning with the League of Nations, international organizations have been set in place that have bred habits of co-operation, and reinforced the message that we should try to avoid war whenever we can. Regional systems such as the European Union have also altered the regional landscape of war and peace. Multilateral regimes have established new normative standards of behaviour. We must always add the rider that one of the reasons why the present system has survived so long is that no great power has been so dissatisfied with prevailing political arrangements and yet strong enough that it has felt any need to embark on a revisionist path like Nazi Germany in the 1930s. Russia is dissatisfied but too weak; China is strong but satisfied for the time being.

But the underlying reality has not changed. As Michael Howard argues, no world order can be

created simply by building international organizations and institutions that do not arise naturally out
of the cultural dispositions or historical experience
of its members.[1] And that is why ultimately the
'endists' always tend to fall back on Kant's optimism
that humanity will become more benign over time.
He was spinning a metanarrative, one of many from
the eighteenth century; in this case that humanity
would achieve 'moral maturity'. It is not at all clear
why this story should be more compelling than any
other, including Aldous Huxley's despairing belief
that humans are still in their infancy and that if we
were to grow up fully we would become brutish
apes (hunched, hairy and sitting in our own faeces),
a theory inspired by his brother Julian's experimen-
tal injection of hormones into axolotls, pink-faced
salamanders with a disconcertingly human appear-
ance.

The real weakness of Kant's proposition is that
he thought the world would grow morally at the
same time because human values were universal.
Western politicians still make this mistake. George
W. Bush expressed this forcefully in a speech at West
Point in June 2002: 'Different circumstances require
different methods, but not different moralities.
Moral truth is the same in every culture, in every
time and in every place.' It was on that understand-

ing that the neo-conservatives went to war with Iraq. Unfortunately, moral truth is not the same everywhere and at all times. Even in Afghanistan, as a NATO spokeswoman admitted (*The Times*, 7 April 2009), 98% of women in Shia areas were in favour of a law that would have effectively legalized rape in marriage, and which the government only withdrew after strong Western protests. The basic assumption of the entire benighted NATO mission is that the Afghans want what it wants, or that they want what it wants them to want. What else is the 'hearts and minds' mission than an attempt to produce what the US military calls 'sustained behavioural change'? In the end, the West has decided to leave the Afghan army to fight it out, not because its goals have been achieved but because it has given up on them.

Philosophical mills grind exceeding small and the aim of philosophy is to show that things are trickier than they might seem to be at first. The point is that there is no universal morality; there are only a series of what Charles Taylor calls 'social imaginaries' that are more or less believable at different times. One of the most potent social imaginaries is the western democratic, which is important also for the 'end of war school', given the contention that democracies don't go to war against each other. At its heart is the vision of a normative order anchored to natural rights whose ends are common benefits, of which the most important is security. The theory of natural rights ends up producing a dense web of limits to legislative and executive action. Presumptions of equality (anchored, in turn, to social contract theory) have permeated our institutions in the form of non-discriminatory legislation and equal opportunity rights. The western social imaginary is an elusive set of self-understandings, practices and expectations which include some very specific western inventions such as the sovereignty of the 'people', who understand themselves to be a self-constituting group that exists prior to the formulation of any formal political set of laws, conventions and customs.[2] Unfortunately, Taylor's work has very little to say about non-western social imaginaries, let alone non-western versions of moral order. And he has almost nothing to say on how social imaginaries and war still feed off each other. For a long time the West has used force to defend human rights; in the 1990s 'humanitarian wars' became quite the fashion.

The western social imaginary with its aggressive secularism could not be more different from the Islamic. The western belief in a secular order emerges in a famous paragraph from *The Philosophy of*

Right (1821) where Hegel tells us that the origin of the modern state as 'a self-organizing rational and ethical organization' can be traced back to the breakdown of religious unity in the West. For ethical constraints no longer came from God, but from within – from politics. The first and most important precondition of the modern concept of the state is the formation of a distinctive language of politics. In other words, for modern politics to be made possible, it was necessary to accept the idea of the state, which presupposed that a political society was held together solely for political purposes. The emergence of the 'political' realm is also associated with the emergence of the 'citizen' in the late eighteenth century (as distinct from the Christian or the subject). Human rights first emerged in the *Declaration of the Rights of Man* (1789) (we tend to omit the all-important subordinate clause '*And the Citizen*'). We often forget that for us the political sphere is both modern and ethical at the same time. Ethics inheres in the political practice of forging and keeping together a state divided by class and other conflicting interests. The aim, claimed Marx, was to create an *illusionische Gemeinschaft* (an illusionary society) held together by certain foundational myths, such as that of the social contract and human rights (neither are objectively real, of course – they are only as real as our willingness to suspend disbelief).

None of this can be squared with the Islamic social imaginary, and this is important. The abstract language of human rights has not translated into a universal human code of conduct, because it has failed to enter into the depth of what Islam means to a Muslim, or Christianity still means to various Christians. As Jonathan Sacks complains, it suggests that the particularities of a culture are mere accretions to our essential and indivisible humanity, instead of being what they really are – the very substance of how most people learn what it is to be human.[3] And it is in the name of our *individuated* humanity that Jihadists join up to fight in Somalia and Syria, just as Garibaldi enlisted in the French war effort in 1870; and many Central European Jewish communists fought and died in the French Resistance; and Spanish Republicans were among the first to liberate Paris in August 1944.

The philosopher John Gray is highly sceptical of any project that posits a single human vision of peace. He is often accused of moral relativism in thinking that there are many ways of life in which humans can best express themselves, and that some of those ways of life may even require war for their expression. He is criticized for believing that it is possible for people to lead self-fulfilled lives very different from our own, but he is surely right. There are no overarching standards whereby the virtues recognized in different cultural traditions can be put in the balance and weighed. 'The virtues of the Homeric epics and of the Sermon on the Mount are irreducibly divergent and conflicting, and they express radically different forms of life. There is no Archimedean point of leverage from which they can be judged.'[4]

I would regard this as an example of moral realism, not relativism. We can question, of course, whether any values are in any sense 'objective'. Philosophically, the most controversial and by far the most radical of the value sceptics was David Hume, who held that if we pursued the 'good' (defined by Aristotle) – and most monotheistic faiths believe God to be good – there is no such thing as objective goodness. Our judgements of right and wrong are just matters of sentiment which we project into the world and imagine constitute part of the fabric of reality. Such moral judgements have nothing to do with objective truth, or even reason. As Hume famously put it in his *Treatise of Human Nature* (1739–40): ''Tis not contrary to reason to prefer the destruction of the whole world to the scratching of my finger.' But those who take the opposite view (as most of us do) accept that values do exist and they are real enough if they reflect our individual interests and concerns, which often differ from culture to culture. What is undoubtedly universal is the idea of value itself. We demand fair treatment and a measure of self-esteem. Both are pro-social values for we are social animals, which is why we all dislike betrayal and disloyalty. As James Q. Wilson argued in *The Moral Sense* (1993), just as children are equipped to learn language, so we come into the world equipped with a specific set of moral prejudices that make us social beings fit for society. And we have these values for a reason; it is one of the central ways we co-ordinate our lives with those of others; we appeal to them whenever we are trying to get things done together. The key insight of modern philosophical reflection is that language has been hard-wired into us – it provides an evaluative tool that helps us work with each other more effectively. It allows us to value a person for being a 'hard worker', or 'devoted mother', and to devalue those we find to be anti-social. Unfortunately, most other values are inherently appraisive, and that just happens to include peace. Indeed, that is why the definition of war and peace is so difficult to construct. As one writer argues, '[W]e reject war because it ruins social relations, shatters bodies and savages human rights. Yet, we also look to war to preserve the social, protect threatened lives and enlarge rights. War kills and saves simultaneously.'[5]

Peace as a contested concept

What do we mean by peace, asked Susan Sontag in her 2001 Jerusalem Prize acceptance speech? Do we mean the absence of strife, or forgetting, or forgiveness, or do we mean the great weariness of exhaustion that often follows a war, which can be accompanied, but not always, by an emptying out of rancour? What most people mean by peace, of course, is victory; the victory of their own side. Calls for peace for the defeated often appear for that reason fraudulent.[6] There are so many different ways in which peace for oneself can mean oppression or marginalization for others. For Sontag there was very little disagreement on the desirability of peace, but there was on its realization, and that is because many disagreements are entirely reasonable, even if different parties may think each other profoundly mistaken.

Kant thought that if you would only employ correct reasoning you could argue anyone out of anything that was 'wrong', and he grounded this belief in Euclidean geometry, the geometry of flat surfaces that we learn in school. Years later mathematicians robbed us of this illusion by demonstrating that non-Euclidean geometry is equally valid – triangles constructed from the shortest lines between three points don't always have interior angles that add up to 180 degrees. It is quite possible, in other words, to have a proposition that is true in one mathematical system and false in another. And this is even truer in our human constructed world for human beings are what they understand themselves to be. We are comprised entirely of beliefs about ourselves and about the world we inhabit.

For that reason many of the things we dream of achieving, including peace, are what the philosopher Walter Bryce Gallie called 'contested concepts'. The example Gallie gave is an interesting one. 'This picture is painted in oils' is either true or false and can be exposed as false if it is painted, actually, in tempera. 'This picture is a work of art' is a quite different proposition since anything can be a work of art, from Duchamp's famous urinal to Jean-Tinguely's habit of setting fire to his own monumental works immediately after completing them. The only way, Gallie suggests, to gain universal agreement would be to coin a new meaning of 'a work of art' to which all disputants could agree; or to force all disputants to accept one meaning; or to declare 'a work of art' to be a number of different concepts employing the same name. If this is impossible when it comes to art, it is equally impossible when it comes to peace.

Imperialism is a vivid example of the second proposal. A peace enforced by an imperial power is often real enough. The *Pax Britannica* was considered a high achievement by the British themselves, but it also involved constant pacification. In the period between 1909 and 1918, during which British authority extended over the Langi people of Northern Uganda (a stateless society), there was only one year in which a punitive expedition was not launched to pacify the region. The third proposal is really a non-starter since it is easier to agree to disagree (what is really being asked of every art critic) on what constitutes a work of art, and the same I would venture is also true of peace. Whatever its imperfections, we can, however, recognize peace, and its costs. The nuclear regime enforced by the two superpowers held for over forty years, but we must never forget that it also made war safe for what we used to call the Third World, in which proxy conflicts abounded. Fifty million people died on the battlefields of the Cold

War – indeed, to call it 'cold' is an insult to their memory.

Moreover, if we were to embrace Gallie's first proposal, we would have to come up with an entirely new meaning of 'peace'. And that would be difficult, argues Gray, because it would require universal values, and if such values don't exist, then peace would be built on shifting sand. Would it be just to ban war while social inequality and injustice are increasing so rapidly? As Hedley Bull argued in *The Anarchical Society* (1976), a disarmed world (a world in which people were not permitted to fight for their freedom, or their rights) would not necessarily be a just world. There are a wide range of conditions called 'war' and conditions called 'peace', contrary to what you find in academic departments, where the two phenomena are bracketed off from each other and taught separately.

Would we ever be fully satisfied with defining peace merely as the absence of war; would we ever be satisfied with such a mere negation of the term? Surely, we would always want it to be something more. Language is never adequate to describe an absolute reality, but can we be at peace with ourselves if we are aware of the injustice of the world around us? Would peace of mind be the result of ignorance or simply disinterest, or just plain inability to empathize with the plight of others?

This is why there is no reason to be dismissive of individual peace settlements whenever they are brokered. If you cannot wage peace in the same way that you wage war, you can at least often attain it by incremental means, and some peace settlements are attained in the most unlikely of circumstances. Back in 2001 one commentator predicted that the conflict in Macedonia was not yet over; the peace deal, he added, was merely a 'post-dated suicide note'. Another declared that the country was poised to erupt – 'rarely has the very process of history been so transparent and crystal'.[7] Macedonia, of course, has been at peace for years; social scientists have a dismally poor record of prediction, which is why you shouldn't believe them when they predict the coming end of war.

6

Humanity

'Nothing to be done' – in Serbian, *Nista ne moze da se uradi* – is the opening line of Samuel Beckett's bleak play *Waiting for Godot*, which Susan Sontag directed in the besieged city of Sarajevo in the summer of 1993. Bleak, perhaps, but was it really more gloomy, she asked, than two other productions that were in rehearsal at the same time – *Alcestis* (a play about the inevitability of death and the meaning of sacrifice) and *Ajax* (a play about a man's madness and suicide)? Sontag quoted Émile Durkheim's words, 'Society is above all the idea it forms of itself.'[1] The idea that Europe had formed of itself by the late twentieth century was that it was anthropologically impossible for Europeans ever again to go to war against each other. In 1990, utterly confounded by the return of war to the Western Balkans, and the siege of the very city where the First World War had been ignited, Western Europe had chosen to turn its back on the atrocities that accompanied the dissolution of the former Yugoslavia. And yet the Bosnian cause was surely Europe's, Sontag wrote, and since the European Union was a society composed of citizens, not members of a tribe, why had these atrocities not aroused a more robust response?

Determined to stay focused on the big picture, I tell this story for a reason. We always return to our evolutionary past – to in-group and out-group dynamics. What Sontag witnessed were a people cut off from the only way of escape that as a species we have – the way forward, into the future. We are a species that at any moment can regress, especially under stress, but we are also the only species to know this. When a writer tells you that you can eliminate a practice as deeply ingrained in the human story as war, you would do well to doubt her objectivity; equally when she tells you that you can't, you are entitled to the same reaction. We have a duty to reject Brecht's despairing belief that human beings learn as much from the catastrophes they themselves bring about as laboratory rabbits learn about biology. Brecht was wrong about most things. It is our ability to learn from history that gives us hope that we can change our behavioural profile.

Perhaps, however, we need to ask quite a different question. Are we too aggressive a species to live without recourse to collective violence; does the fault lie in our evolved biology? Let me invoke one of the most famous correspondences of the twentieth century, which began when Einstein sent Freud a letter in September 1932 asking whether humanity could ever be liberated from the threat of war. Like many others at the time, Einstein thought that only in 'the psychological development of man' could we invest any hope that war would be eliminated (just as Kant invested so much faith in man's moral maturity). He assumed that war was the product of irrationality. In his reply, Freud fell back on his own first principles. *Eros* could overcome *thanatos* (the death instinct) if there was a 'strengthening of intellect' against our innate aggressive instincts. Modern humans, for the first time, at least, recognized the destructiveness of war, even though they could not always act on that understanding. But Freud was not optimistic by nature or philosophical disposition. To be chronically ill, he once wrote, was part of what it is to be human. Privately, he even considered the exchange with Einstein to be 'tedious and sterile', in part because, like Kant, he thought of himself as an 'unworldly theoretician'.[2]

But unwarranted pessimism can be dangerous,

too. Take the 'return of the repressed', in itself a somewhat dispiriting doctrine. Freud believed that a person who becomes the victim of a violent action (such as sexual abuse) may repress the memory for years, often over a lifetime. One day, however, it may rise to the surface of the conscious mind. When it does so, the reaction can be cathartic: through counselling, the patient can come to terms with the experience and may even forgive the perpetrator. Others will not be so forgiving. And just a few will wish to take their revenge, usually through the law courts. More recently we have seen an alarming variation – 'recovered memory syndrome'. Therapists, in their zeal to find child abusers or molesters, unintentionally 'plant' in children's minds a false memory of abuse. The emotional costs to all involved are staggering. In Orkney in the early 1990s many children were taken away from their parents because under examination they imagined they had been the victims of satanic rites. So, on the Freudian model (translated from the individual to an entire traumatized society), the memory of an historical injustice does not have to be real, it only has to be imagined. And the people who place this in the mind are not therapists, but politicians like Tudjman and Milošević.

The popularity of Freudian ideas had much to

do with the intellectual climate of the inter-war and post-war years, which was a response to the 'madness' of both world wars. Freudianism, however, was not the only movement impressed by the apparent irrational side of human nature. In the case of Yugoslavia, the story went as follows. When in 1941 the Germans invaded, what followed was not a partisan struggle against the occupying power so much as a murderous civil war among the Yugoslavs themselves: Croats against Serbs, and both against Bosnians and Montenegrins. When the Communists came to power, these memories were suppressed in the name of national unity; when Communism collapsed, the repressed memories returned. The nationalists exploited them. It helped that after the Second World War many Yugoslavs had not handed in their guns but returned with them to their farms and livelihoods, prepared and ready for the next conflict.

If you believe such stories, you would be a fool not to take them seriously. President Clinton was so convinced that the ethnic cleansing was the outcome of 500 years of resentments and pent-up hatreds that it materially affected his decision not to get involved in the Balkans until much later on, after most of the damage had been done. The good news is that recovered memories do not provoke people to go to war. Researchers at the McLean Hospital (affiliated with the Harvard Medical School) recently conducted a research project which found that recovered memory cannot be traced back beyond the nineteenth century, in the form of either fiction or fact. The phenomenon, in other words, is not a natural neurological function, but 'a culture-bound syndrome' rooted in nineteenth-century romanticism.[3] So we can ditch it, together with many other discredited concepts such as Freud's 'death wish' and Erich Fromm's 'catastrophe complex', and much else by way of pseudo-scientific or pseudo-psychological explanations which *pathologize* war (and thus the human condition).

Beyond false memories, Freud also claimed that we are driven by aggressive instincts, a claim that he developed in his book *The Future of an Illusion* (1927). But this too is doubtful. We are innately aggressive, no doubt, but the trait will develop only in a specific set of circumstances, though when it does so it can be disturbing. Take the Senai, a tribe in Malaya who came closest to Rousseau's myth of primal innocence. In their society, killing was largely unknown; they didn't even have a word for it. But when they were recruited by the British in the 1950s to fight in the anti-communist struggle, they seem to have been swept away by a collective insanity which they themselves called 'blood drunkenness'. As a general rule, however, we are far less aggressive than any other species, such as chimpanzees. Our aggression is focused. Unlike lions or hyenas, our violence is rarely lethal on an individual basis. What is particularly depressing is the current tendency to devalue our humanity by insisting that there is no difference between us and the higher primates. In fact, there is a lot, especially when it comes to violence. As Edward O. Wilson contends in *On Human Nature* (1978), if baboons had nuclear weapons, they would have destroyed the world in a week.

Sportive monsters

Still is the bottom of the sea: who would guess that it harbours sportive monsters?
> Nietzsche, *Thus Spake Zarathustra*, Part 2
> ('Of the Sublime Men')

So if war is not pathological, and if we are not murderously aggressive, why is peace so elusive?

A clue can be found in Michael Howard's book *The Invention of Peace* (2001), which ends on a profoundly pessimistic note. War is not going to end, and his explanation, most would agree, is surprising. Peaceful societies are boring. The vast majority of humanity, he reminds us, never had enough leisure to experience boredom, which is why the word itself did not appear in fiction until Charles Dickens' novel *Bleak House* (1853). It is in our nature to escape from boredom, sometimes even into war. For Fukuyama, peace has its entropic principles, too. If you cannot struggle for a just cause, you may choose to struggle against one. '[We] will struggle, in other words, out of boredom, [for] we cannot imagine living in a world without struggle.'[4]

Boredom is not what many suppose it to be: a lack of concentration or interest in life. It involves a lack of agency. People are bored when they feel powerless to do anything. Take a young white lower-middle-class youth from New York sidelined by history, or two young Muslims in Boston with few opportunities for self-expression, and frequently under- if not unemployed. Both have a strong sense of resentment, like Tim McVeigh, or Tamerlan and Dzhokhar Tsarnaev, the Boston Marathon bombers. Engaging in crime is the most obvious remedy; but terrorism is becoming increasingly popular. And so too is torture, to which the white lower-middle-class jailers in Abu Ghraib resorted to combat the numbing boredom of prison duty. Torture, after all, is the ultimate act of transgression, an affirmation of agency (we have power, you do not). It is the perfect antidote to boredom.

There are many telling fictional examples of these coping strategies. One is Chuck Palahniuk's novel *Fight Club* (1996), also a popular film, a searing satire in which the protagonist becomes so disgusted at American consumerism that he joins an underground terrorist organization dedicated to destroying credit card companies. The ultimate rationale for his behaviour is that he wants 'a near-life experience'. A terrorist in Don DeLillo's novel *Players* (1974) wants to blow up the New York Stock Exchange so as to 'organize the emptiness'. That emptiness is captured in Bret Easton Ellis's novel *American Psycho* (1991), where the murderous protagonist rebels against the Wall Street Yuppie lifestyle by randomly killing women at night. When asked what he does by a girl in a nightclub, he replies in all deviant honesty, 'Oh, murders and executions mostly.' She mistakes this for 'mergers and acquisitions'. It is the protagonist's particular misfortune that even his own transgressive acts go unrecognized by the society he loathes.

None of which is to claim that transgressive behaviour produces war, but it is to suggest that war both cultivates and brings it out and that it may later feed back into the way war is conducted. It opens the doors to the evil among us, and sometimes the evil within us too. This is another of war's dialectical relationships, which is grounded in the fact that we are a game-playing species: *Homo Ludens*, to cite Johann Huizinga's famous 1938 book. As Judge Holden remarks in Cormac McCarthy's novel *Blood Meridian* (1985), war is the ultimate game because we play for keeps; it is a 'forcing of the unity of existence'. It is the most rewarding game of all, for those who want to play it.

But, 'here is the thing, professor', my students might now say: *who* is actually in control? For Hans-Georg Gadamer, '[T]he game masters the players; ... the real subject of the game ... is not the players, but the game itself.'[5] And this is especially true of video games which encourage subversive behaviour. Their great cult heroes are Nietzsche's 'sportive monsters' – the players who have found a way to break the rules. Players of Eve Online still celebrate the covert 'assassin guild' which killed the leader of a major in-game corporation and stole its assets. In Halo a method called 'warthog-jumping' was soon discovered which allowed players to propel their avatars high into the air and thereby access parts of the landscape that were meant to be out of bounds.[6] Most disturbing of all, perhaps, is World of Warcraft. What began as a game took on the sharp contours of a life that was apparently real enough for some players. For something happened in 2005 that the programmers had not anticipated: some players began teleporting themselves through portals in time to enemy societies where they infected the inhabitants with a deadly biological virus. The virus spread so quickly that the manufacturers were forced to pull the plug and reboot the system. Quite soon it also came to the notice of the Department of Homeland Security, which was fascinated that some players were willing to sacrifice themselves for others by becoming suicide-terrorists.

The human predicament

From the perspective of the evolutionary biologist we will never eliminate violence, individual or collective, because there are limits to how much we can change. Evolutionary thought isn't totally pessimistic, but it has dashed the great Enlightenment hope in 'the perfectibility of Man' and replaced it with an unashamedly realistic view of what may yet be achieved. Our world only began 11,000 years ago when we first became herders and settlers rather than hunter-gatherers. A few thousand years later we began to form states; a little later we began to join Facebook. This is a significantly short time in the history of our species. Our skulls are still lumbered with Stone Age brains that are maladapted to modern life; we still disregard long-term threats because we are hard-wired to take more urgent note of short-term concerns. Humanity is said to have emerged from the Pleistocene socially adapted for the transformation to come; but it has still not done so in terms of Kantian moral progress.

This is why Steven Pinker's *The Better Angels of Our Nature* (2012), with its paean to human progress, met with a hostile response in some quarters. Seven thousand years of history are covered in breathless haste; human prehistory runs to only two pages of a 700-page book. Pinker was merely taking further Norbert Elias' great work *The Civilizing Process* (1939), which charted in minute detail the growth of internal and external constraints on aggressive behaviour – the decline of duelling and its honour codes, and feudalism and its private armies. In a word, *modernity* makes us less violent with the aid of mutually reinforcing projects such as democratic participation, economic interdependence and constructive conflict resolution. It is a cumulative process that is difficult to reverse – except that it really isn't.

In *The Blank Slate* (2006) Pinker was much more pessimistic. The grasp of our own humanity is still pretty rudimentary, which is why even genetic engineering is probably not the answer. Elsewhere Pinker even went so far as to suggest that philosophy is, in part, the application of a mental tool to problems that it was not designed to solve.[7] Evolutionary psychologists tend to be pessimistic about Kantian dreams of moral uplift for that reason; they recognize that we are what we are and there may be a limit to what we might yet 'become'.

We call it the human condition. We must accept that though we are animals we are unlike every other species because we are unfinished animals at our birth. For the rest of our life we are subject to impressions and sensations and sights that lead from time to time to useful insights into our own condition. The world is one of beliefs filtered through by culture, and different cultures produce different emotional repertoires, as they do ways of warfare. And we are always at the mercy of cognitive dissonance, a deeply disturbing reminder of how what we take for reality is under-determined by objective factors on which we think wrongly that our taking is based. We are hard-wired to be prejudiced against others and biased in favour of the in-group (people like us). We really are 'wired' to distinguish ourselves from other people, even at the most prosaic level. Charlton Heston, the star of the first *Planet of the Apes* (1968) movie, tells us that the ape performers sat separately at lunchtime, self-segregating by species – gorillas at one table, chimps at another and orangutans at still a third. Heston would later quip: 'I leave it to the anthropologists to figure this out.'

If we are still waiting for them to report back, social psychologists have helped to fill in some of the blanks. When objective reality challenges our beliefs, we don't always change them – 'confirmation bias' allows us to be even more convinced in the rightness of our original judgements of other people (especially people unlike us). It even sees to it that no evidence – or absence of evidence – is convincing evidence for what we have believed all along. In short, the real problem is not that we are a particularly irredeemable species but that we don't have ultimate control over our thoughts and therefore our actions. We may never eliminate war for that reason; its possibility gives us, at least, an illusion of being in control.

And as long as we continue to tell stories which make us fearful of one another, we will continue to 'game' for all eventualities. Will Storr insists that all such stories are profoundly useful in helping us to co-operate with each other while being often highly dangerous at the same time.[8] If you want it otherwise, you may not have to wait long. In Jack Williamson's story 'With Folded Arms' (1947), an army of robots programmed to protect people from harm end up enslaving them. With tyrannical benef-icence they refuse to allow humanity to perform any significant activity since even the most trivial can provoke dissension.[9] We have been warned. Robots are on the way, as science fiction writers have been anticipating since the 1930s. And we should remember science fiction sets out not so much to explore the possibilities of the future as to comment on the crises that it sees imminent in contemporary life.

The evolution of free will

In Tom Stoppard's play *Travesties* (1974) the nar-rator dreams he is cross-examining James Joyce and asks triumphantly: 'What did *you* do in the war?' 'I wrote *Ulysses*,' Joyce replies. 'What did *you* do?' Joyce spent much of the war in Zurich, as did Lenin – a remarkable coincidence that inspired Stoppard to write his play. It would be comforting to think that one day we will not have wars, so such questions will never have to be asked again. It would be even more comforting to think that one day we will consider a novel like *Ulysses* more important than a war. But that day is some way off.

Unlike war, peace is an idea (or, as Howard writes, an 'invention'), and like all ideas it depends on the choices we make, given that we are the only species on the planet to enjoy free will. Kant put a challenge to the philosophers of his day – and ours. We are free to choose, a truth he felt to be so intuitively self-evident that no-one could argue that freedom away. His argument for free will was actually a religious one, for it is only free will that enables God to watch us grow morally, and Kant, of course, wagered on our moral improvement over time. Is it so unreasonable to imagine a world different from what it is; and that we might play a large part in making it different? Or is it possible to make any genuinely independent choices if we are merely a cluster of cells and genes in a world determined by scientific laws?

Rather surprisingly, perhaps, Daniel Dennett argues against the current fashion that our future is fixed because our nature is. Neither, he insists, is actually true. We are continuing to evolve, and are probably evolving faster through digital media than we have since we first learned to read. We are still the only species plastic in its possibilities. Free will does exist, but instead of being an unchanging, eternal condition of our existence, it has evolved too, and is continuing to do so. Dennett puts it very well. We see inevitabilities in our lives but the list is getting smaller. Our world is becoming more *evitable*.[10] And what is evitable is open to human interference and agency. Let me provide a concrete example. We will probably never achieve a nuclear-free world, but we could, if we so choose, adopt Paul Doty's proposal (outlined in an article in *Daedalus* in the Fall of 2009) to reduce the number of nuclear weapons so that we no longer have the power to destroy civilization, even though we may still be able to wipe out individual countries. As a former member of the Manhattan Project, Doty should be listened to. The trouble is that once we talk of evitability, we must also acknowledge the possibilities of developing smaller nuclear bombs such as 'bunker busters' and thus entering 'the second nuclear age' ahead of the field.

It was Aristotle who first said it is only worth discussing what is within our power. Until very recently we had very little power to change our circumstances. It is possible that our circumstances could change radically, not least because of our capacity to reason out how we might be more 'fit for purpose'. But, of course, we also have the freedom to reason out how we might wage war even more effectively in the future. The problem in the end is free will itself.

So let me sum up. I have argued that war is continuing to evolve, and that until such time as it reaches an evolutionary dead-end we are more likely than not to remain in the war business. If its cultural enhancers are still strong, if not stronger than ever; if technology still 'wants' war, but in ways that suggest we may increasingly have to see it from the machine's point of view (to privilege logic over reason); if the state still remains the supreme political entity, now once again adapting to a changed environment; if we will continue to spin geopolitical narratives that may take us into uncharted territory; and if our moral values are less universal than we think, then it seems eccentric in the extreme to write off war quite yet. As George Kennan, one of the wisest of political commentators, once wrote, war cannot be banned by specific treaties or charters agreed upon in a single moment of history and reflecting only the outlooks and circumstances of that particular moment. War lies too deeply buried 'in the ingrained habits and assumptions of men'.[11]

If the 'endists' want to be more persuasive, they will have to come up with better arguments, and I hope this study will stimulate them to do precisely that. Otherwise, we are left with only a series of Just-So stories derived from the Enlightenment which are only as 'real' as the imagination holding them together. Blind optimism is not the answer, but nor is despairing pessimism. Even so, I am the first to admit, the message of this book is not all that forgiving. 'Man hands on misery to man. It deepens like a coastal shelf,' Philip Larkin wrote rather gloomily in 1971. Whether the coastal shelf is as deep today as it was then, we remain linked to our prehistoric past, so much so that, like Kennan, I believe we are unlikely any time soon to witness a major change of heart.

Further Reading

Readers wanting to broaden the analysis in Chapter 1 and read more about the evolution of war would do well to consult David Livingstone Smith, *The Most Dangerous Animal: Human Nature and the Origins of War* (New York: St Martin's Press, 2007) and Paul Crook, *Darwinism, War and History* (Cambridge: Cambridge University Press, 1994). The best defence of group selection is David Sloan-Wilson, 'Re-introducing group selection to the human behavioral sciences' (*http://socio.ch/evo/sobwil.html*, accessed 20 June 2013). For an historical overview of war's evolving complexity, see Azar Gat, *War in Human Civilization* (Oxford: Oxford University Press, 2007). For the complexity of non-state acts of warfare today, see John Robb, *Brave New War* (Hoboken, NJ: John Wiley & Sons, 2007). For the problems of the western way of war, see John France, *Perilous Glory* (New Haven, CT: Yale University Press, 2011). For the future of military urbanism, see Stephen Graham, *Cities under Siege* (London: Verso, 2010).

Chapter 2's analysis of culture relies heavily on Mark Pagel, *Wired for Culture: The Natural History of Human Co-operation* (London: Allen Lane, 2012). The most persuasive discussion is Barbara Ehrenreich, *Blood Rites: The Origins and History of the Passions of War* (London: Virago, 1997). Two of the best books on the warrior experience as a 'religious' phenomenon are Sebastian Junger, *War* (New York: HarperCollins, 2010) and Karl Marlantes, *What's It Like to Go to War?* (London: Corvus, 2011). For a general history of women and war, see Malcolm Potts and Thomas Hayden, *Sex and War* (Dallas: Ben Bella, 2009).

A more general coverage of Chapter 3's analysis of technology is to be found in Timothy Taylor, *The Artificial Ape: How Technology Changed the Course of Human Evolution* (London: Palgrave, 2010). For an analysis of war's impact on human cognition, see John Ellis, *The Social History of the Machine Gun* (London: Pimlico, 1993) and Antoine Bousquet, *The Scientific Way of Warfare* (London: Hurst, 2009). For the onset of post-human war, see my *Warrior Geeks: How 21st Century Technology is Changing the Way We Fight and Think About War* (London: Hurst, 2013). The best book on robots in still Peter Singer, *Wired for War* (New York: Penguin, 2009). For a sceptical view of cyber-war, see Thomas Rid, *Cyberwar Will Not Take Place* (London: Hurst, 2013).

For a wider discussion of classical geopolitics broached in Chapter 4, see Colin Gray, *Another Bloody Century* (London: Weidenfeld & Nicolson, 2005). For a critique of both critical geopolitics and traditional geopolitics, see Phil Kelly, 'A critique of critical geopolitics', *Geopolitics*, 11:1 (2006). On globalization and the state, see Erik Gartzke 'The capitalist peace', *The American Journal of Political Science*, 51 (January 2007), pp. 166–93. For nuclear weapons, see Ron Rosenbaum, *How the End Begins* (New York: Simon & Schuster, 2011). Finally, on the 'impossibility' of Great Power War, see Michael Mandelbaum, 'Is major war obsolete?', *Survival*, 40:4 (Winter 1998–9). For a refutation of these views, see my *The Coming of War with China* (London: Hurst, in press) and Edward Luttwak, *The Rise of China versus the Logic of Strategy* (Cambridge, MA: Harvard University Press, 2012). There is a growing literature on climate change and the onset of war: see James Arlee, *Climate Change and Armed Conflict: Hot and Cold Wars* (London:

Routledge, 2009) and Paul Hirst, *War and Power in the 21st Century* (Cambridge: Polity, 2001).

The case for non-violence, discussed in Chapter 5, can be found in John Horgan, *The End of War* (San Francisco: McSweeney Books, 2012). John Gray's work includes *Enlightenment's Wake* (London: Routledge, 1995). William Gallie's work on contested concepts can be found in *Philosophy and Historical Understanding* (London: Chatto and Windus, 2004). The best book on why peace is possible is John Gittings, *The Glorious Arts of Peace* (Oxford: Oxford University Press, 2012). As a corrective see Matthew Hughes and Matthew Seligmann, *Does Peace Lead to War?* (Stroud: Sutton Press, 2002).

Chapter 6 touches only briefly on the evolutionary psychologists' view of war. The best book is Jonathan Gottschall, *The Rape of Troy: Evolution, Violence and the World of Homer* (Cambridge: Cambridge University Press, 2011). On Freud and Einstein's correspondence, see Russell Jacoby, *Blood Lust: On the Route to Violence from Cain and Abel to the Present* (New York: Simon & Schuster, 2011). For an inveterately optimistic take on our growing tendency towards non-violence, see Steven Pinker, *The Better Angels of Our Nature* (London: Penguin Books, 2012). For a more realistic understanding of our destiny, see Cormac McCarthy's novel *Blood Meridian* (London: Picador, 2010) and its discussion in my book *Men at Arms: What Fiction Has to Tell Us About Conflict from Achilles to Flashman* (London: Hurst, 2013).

Notes

Prologue

1 Jon Ronson, *The Men Who Stare at Goats* (London: Picador, 2002), p. 1.
2 E.D. Dames and Joel Henry, *Now Tell Me What You See* (Hoboken, NJ: John Wiley & Sons, 2011).
3 Barbara Ehrenreich, *Blood Rites: The Origins and History of the Passions of War* (London: Virago, 1997), p. 235.
4 John Keegan, *War and Our World* (London: Hutchinson 1998), p. 72.
5 Andrew Zolli and Ann-Marie Healy, *Resilience: Why Things Bounce Back* (London: Headline, 2012), pp. 6–7.

Chapter 1 Evolution

1 David Sloan-Wilson, *Darwin's Cathedral: Evolution, Religion and the Nature of Society* (Chicago: University of Chicago Press, 2007).

2 Matt Ridley, *The Rational Optimist* (London: Fourth Estate, 2011), p. 44.

3 Robert Wright, *The Evolution of God* (London: Little & Brown, 2009), p. 79.

4 Mary Midgley, *The Solitary Self* (London: Acumen, 2010).

5 Cited in Catherine Belsey, 'Biology and imagination: the role of culture', in Robin Headlam Wells and Johnjoe McFadden (eds), *Human Nature: Fact and Fiction* (London: Continuum, 2006), p. 116.

6 David Samuels, 'Q&A: Edward Luttwak', *Tablet*, 6 September 2011: *http://www.tabletmag.com/jewish-news-and-politics/76739/qa-edward-luttwak?all=1* (accessed 20 June 2013).

7 Cited in Kevin Kelly, *What Technology Wants* (New York: Penguin, 2010), p. 305.

8 Max Brooks, *World War Z: An Oral History of the Zombie War* (London: Duckworth, 2006).

9 Daniel Dennett, *Freedom Evolves* (London: Penguin, 2003), p. 181.

10 Mark Pagel, *Wired for Culture: The Natural History of Human Co-operation* (London: Allen Lane, 2012).

11 Autulio Echevarria, 'Beyond generations: breaking the cycle', in Karl Erik Haug and Ole Jorgen Maao, *Conceptualising Modern War* (London: Hurst, 2011), p. 56.

12 Andrew Bacevich, 'The Islamic way of war', *American Conservative* 11 (September 2006).

13 Michael Howard, *The Causes of War and Other Essays*, 2nd edn (Cambridge, MA: Harvard University Press, 1984), pp. 214–15.

14 J.R. William McNeill, *The Human Web* (New York: W.W. Norton & Co, 2003), p. 321.
15 Zolli and Healy, *Resilience*, p. 68.
16 Peter Singer, *Wired for War* (New York: Penguin, 2009), pp. 290–1.

Chapter 2 Culture

1 Oona Strathern, *A Brief History of the Future* (London: Robinson, 2007), p. 278.
2 Ehrenreich, *Blood Rites*, p. 235.
3 John Mueller, *War and Ideas* (London: Routledge, 2011), p. 5.
4 Misha Glenny, *McMafia: A Journey through the Global Criminal Underworld* (London: Bodley Head, 2008), p. 123.
5 Jeremy Rifkin, *The Emphatic Civilization* (London: Penguin, 2009), p. 313.
6 Cited in Ian McEwan, 'Literature, science and human nature', in Wells and McFadden (eds), *Human Nature*, p. 38.
7 D.H. Durham, *Co-evolution: Genes, Culture, and Human Diversity* (Stanford: Stanford University Press, 1991).
8 Pagel, *Wired for Culture*, p. 29.
9 Kenneth Pargement, *The Psychology of Religion* (New York: Guilford, 1997).
10 Cited in David Sloan-Wilson, 'Why Richard Dawkins is wrong about religion', in Alex Bentley (ed.), *The Edge of Reason? Science and Religion in Modern Society* (London: Continuum, 2008), p. 133.

11 David Andress, *The Savage Storm: Britain on the Brink in the Age of Napoleon* (New York: Little, Brown, 2012), p. 121.

12 Jonathan Gotschall, *The Story-telling Animal: How Stories Make Us Human* (New York: Houghton-Mifflin-Harcourt, 2012).

13 Jared Diamond, *The World until Yesterday* (New York: Viking, 2011), pp. 143–4.

14 Shlomo Avineri, 'The problem of war in Hegel's thought', in Jon Stewart (ed.), *The Hegel Myths and Legends* (Evanston, IL: Northwestern University Press, 1996), p. 131.

15 Pagel, *Wired for Culture*, p. 159.

Chapter 3 Technology

1 Kelly, *What Technology Wants*, p. 192.

2 Pagel, *Wired for Culture*, p. 131.

3 Thomas Rid and Peter McBurney, 'Cyberweapons', *RUSI Journal*, 157:1 (February/March 2012), p. 12.

4 Cited Steven Mithen, *The Prehistory of the Mind* (London: Phoenix, 1996), p. 258.

5 Susan Greenfield, *You and Me: The Neuroscience of Identity* (London: Notting Hill Editions, 2011).

6 Isaiah Berlin, *Enlightening Letters 1946–60* (ed. Henry Hardy and Jennifer Holmes) (London: Chatto and Windus, 2009), p. 341.

7 Ronald Arkin, *Governing Lethal Behavior in Autonomous Robots* (Boca Raton, FL: Taylor & Francis, 2009), p. 43.

8 John Markoff, 'War machines: recruiting robots for

combat', *New York Times*, 27 November 2010: *http:// www.nytimes.com/2010/11/28/science/28robot. html?_r=1andem=etal* (accessed 17 June 2013).

9 Cited in Kenan Malik, 'In defence of human agency', in Kurt Almqvist (ed.), *Consciousness, Genetics and Society* (Stockholm: Axel and Margaret Ax:son Johnson Foundation, 2003), p. 179.

10 Cited in Emile Simpson, *War from the Ground Up: Twenty-First Century Combat as Politics* (London: Hurst, 2012) p. 239.

11 Bryan Appleyard, *The Brain is Wider Than the Sky* (London: Weidenfeld & Nicolson, 2011), p. 253.

12 John Updike, *Towards the End of Time* (London: Penguin, 1997), p. 40.

Chapter 4 Geopolitics

1 Leszek Kołokowski, *The Presence of Myth* (Chicago: University of Chicago Press, 1996), p. 31.

2 David Held and Andrew McGrew, 'The end of the old order? Globalization and the prospects for world order', *Review of International Studies*, 24 (1998), p. 222.

3 Cited in Robert Wright, *Non-Zero: The Logic of Human Destiny* (London: Vintage, 2001), p. 38.

4 Niall Ferguson, *The Pity of War* (London: Allen Lane, 1999), p. 23.

5 Richard Rosencrance, *The Rise of the Trading State: Conquest and Commerce in the Modern World* (New York: Basic Books, 1986).

6 Juan Cardinal and Heriberto Araujo, *China's Silent Army* (London: Allen Lane, 2013).

7 Philip Bobbitt, *The Shield of Achilles* (New York: Random House, 2002), p. 308.

8 Ibid.

9 Zolli and Healy, *Resilience*, p. 73.

10 Northrop Frye, *Fearful Symmetry: A Study of William Blake* (Princeton, NJ: Princeton University Press, 1947), p. 264.

11 Robert Kaplan, *The Revenge of Geography* (New York: Random House, 2012), p. 29.

12 Dominique Moisi, *The Geopolitics of Emotions* (New York, Anchor, 2009).

13 Ron Rosenbaum, *How the End Begins* (New York: Simon & Schuster, 2011).

14 Marc Augé, *Non-Places: An Introduction to Supermodernity* (London: Verso, 2008).

15 Jay Kinney, 'Is there a new political paradigm lurking in cyberspace?', in Ziauddin Sardar and Jerome R. Ravetz (eds), *Cyberfutures: Culture and Politics on the Information Superhighway* (London: Pluto Press, 1996), p. 146.

16 Everett C. Dolman, *Astropolitik: Classical Geopolitics in the Space Age* (London: Frank Cass, 2002), p. 4.

Chapter 5 Peace

1 Michael Howard, *The Invention of Peace and the Reinvention of War* (London: Profile Books, 2002), p. 105.

2 Charles Taylor, *A Secular Age* (Cambridge, MA: Harvard University Press, 2007).

3 Jonathan Sacks, *The Dignity of Difference* (London: Continuum, 2002), p. 62.

4 John Gray, *Isaiah Berlin* (Glasgow: Fontana Press, 1995), p. 24.

5 Nick Mansfield, *Theorizing War: From Hobbes to Badiou* (London: Palgrave Macmillan, 2008), p. 163.

6 Susan Sontag, *At the Same Time* (London: Penguin, 2007), p. 145.

7 Robert Kaplan, 'History's cauldron', *Atlantic Monthly*, 267 (June 1991).

Chapter 6 Humanity

1 Susan Sontag, *Where the Stress Falls* (London: Vintage, 2003), p. 326.

2 Cited in Russell Jacoby, *Blood Lust: On the Route to Violence from Cain and Abel to the Present* (New York: Simon & Schuster, 2011), p. 149.

3 Margaret Macmillan, *The Uses and Abuses of History* (London: Profile, 2010), pp. 45–6.

4 Francis Fukuyama, *The End of History and the Last Man* (London: Penguin, 1992), p. 330.

5 Hans-Georg Gadamer, *Truth and Method* (New York: Continuum, 2011), p. 106.

6 Espen Aarseth, 'I fought the law: transgressive play and the implied player', Situated Play, Proceedings of DiGRA 2007 Conference (Centre for Computer Games, 2007), p. 132: *http://www.digra.org/wp-*

content/uploads/digital-library/07313.03489.pdf
(accessed 20 June 2013).

7 Steven Pinker, 'The biology of fiction', in Wells and
  McFadden (eds), *Human Nature*, p. 32.

8 Will Storr, *The Heretics* (London: Picador, 2013), p.
  380.

9 Adam Roberts, *Alien Encounters* (Cambridge, MA:
  Harvard University Press, 1981), p. 165.

10 Dennett, *Freedom Evolves*, p. 54.

11 George Kennan, *The Nuclear Delusion* (New York,
   Norton, 1982), p. xxix.